Autumn Gospel

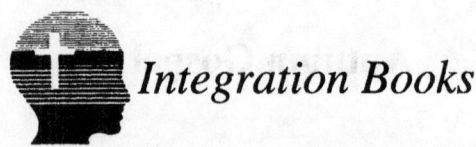 *Integration Books*

STUDIES IN PASTORAL PSYCHOLOGY, THEOLOGY, AND SPIRITUALITY
Robert J. Wicks, General Editor

also in the series

Clinical Handbook of Pastoral Counseling, Volume 1, edited by R. Wicks, R. Parsons, and D. Capps

Adolescents in Turmoil, Parents Under Stress by Richard D. Parsons

Pastoral Marital Therapy by Stephen Treat and Larry Hof

The Art of Clinical Supervision edited by B. Estadt, J. Compton, and M. Blanchette

The Art of Passingover by Francis Dorff, O. Praem.

Losses in Later Life by R. Scott Sullender

Spirituality and Personal Maturity by Joann Wolski Conn

Christointegration by Bernard J. Tyrrell

Choosing Your Career, Finding Your Vocation by Roy Lewis

Adult Children of Alcoholics by Rea McDonnell and Rachel Callahan

Pastoral Care Emergencies by David K. Switzer

Health Care Ministry edited by Helen Hayes and Cornelius J. van der Poel

Surviving in Ministry edited by Robert R. Lutz and Bruce T. Taylor

Renewal in Late Life Through Pastoral Counseling by James N. Lapsley

Clinical Handbook of Pastoral Counseling, Volume 2, edited by R. Wicks and R. Parsons

A Minister's Handbook of Mental Disorders by Joseph W. Ciarrocchi

Human Relationships and the Experience of God by Michael St. Clair

The Psychology of Religion for Ministry by H. Newton Malony

The Doubting Disease by Joseph W. Ciarrocchi

Spiritual Direction in the Dominican Tradition by Benedict M. Ashley, O.P.

Autumn Gospel

Women in the Second Half of Life

Kathleen Fischer

Integration Books

paulist press/new york/mahwah

Other Books by the Author

The Inner Rainbow • Winter Grace • Women at the Well

Other Books by the Author with Thomas N. Hart

The First Two Years of Marriage • Christian Foundations • Promises to Keep •
A Counselor's Prayer Book

Cover design by James F. Brisson.
Interior illustrations by Katherine Malmsten are used with permission.

Library of Congress Cataloging-in-Publication Data

Fischer, Kathleen R., 1940–
Autumn gospel : women in the second half of life / Kathleen Fischer.
   p. cm.—(Integration books)
Includes bibliographical references.
ISBN 0-8091-3581-7 (alk. paper)
   1. Middle aged women—Religious life. 2. Aged women—Religious life. 3. Spiritual life—Christianity. I. Title. II. Series.
BV4579.5.F57   1995
248.8′43—dc20   95-7819
                                                                  CIP

Published by Paulist Press, 997 Macarthur Boulevard, Mahwah, New Jersey 07430

Printed and bound in the United States of America

Contents

Guide to Prayer and Reflection

Foreword

Autumn Gospel is a poetic and informative psychospiritual journey of discovery for women in the second half of life. In this book by Kathleen Fischer, author of **Women at the Well**, there is an invitation for women to: greet and embrace liberating self-images, honor diversity, prize new models of human development, and reclaim women's spiritual power.

In reading **Autumn Gospel** I found myself encouraged and excited anew to seek and recognize the "crone" (wise woman) in each of the mature women in my life. I think women reading this book will not only do this as well, but also learn better ways to appreciate the amazing crone within themselves.

In her treatment of the topic of "transitions" Kathleen Fischer points out the place of discernment and simplicity as well as the need for courage, hope, and a special sensitivity to the "emergence of the new" during periods of change. Following this, she then gives attention to the role of solitude, meditation, and journaling in living a fruitful life as a mature woman. She does this in such an honest and gentle fashion that you know she has both carefully listened to the stories of other women and respectfully fathomed her own life history as well.

Her suggestions on meditative writing are especially helpful. They are practical, clear and even for the experienced journaler a good outline to reflect upon in structuring one's writing about experiences, dreams, and personal feelings.

In the chapter she entitles "The Ways of Wisdom" the topics of attention, awareness, and action are addressed as essential cornerstones necessary in learning to experience in a more sensitive way the quality of "Sophia" (Wisdom). In this chapter, in order to confront interior erroneous hypercritical messages and the darkness of life in general, she invites women to open up new ways to be connected with God and all creation.

In her discussion of the paradox of aging ("Interior awareness often becomes richer while physical abilities slowly lessen.") and in looking at the dynamics of grief, I found her comments once again to simultaneously provide good psychological commonsense information and sound spirituality upon which to reflect.

Finally, **Autumn Gospel** is closed with three fitting chapters: "Remembrance and Redemption," "Giving and Receiving Care," and "Legacies." In the first of these chapters, Kathleen Fischer invites women to revisit their lives with a sense of compassion, forgiveness, and vision. In the next chapter she then offers a realistic and hopeful appraisal of what it means and how it feels to both give and receive care. In it problems such as resentment and misunderstanding take their place alongside the goals of balance and widening our circle of support. Once again, as in the other chapters in this book, the material is clear, rich, and sensitive.

In the closing chapter, we are treated to a discussion of what it means to fathom one's own spiritual legacy. In keeping with this theme, we read of the value of becoming aware of spiritual inheritance and the oftentimes forgotten role of grace-filled mentoring for women in the second half of their lives.

As I finished this chapter and closed the book, I was torn by two feelings. First, I reflected with sadness on how society often tries to set aside the crones in the autumn of their lives, and how we need to do all we can to be countercultural in this respect to prevent this from continuing to happen. And two, I was filled with a sense of joy that someone like Kathleen Fischer is pointing to the "bright colors" of this season in women's lives so they as well as others can rejoice and benefit from a new appreciation of Sophia embodied in them. I think you are really going to like this book.

Robert J. Wicks
Series Editor

Introduction

A friend recently described a walk she and a companion took one evening in late September. They were among tall trees and, from the high cottonwoods, a few leaves would occasionally come loose and float to the ground. Some of the leaves were still green and lush; others were drying up and falling away. "How like a woman's life," she said. As the light moved through the trees, it revealed patterns of intricate beauty. There was something different about this light, my friend said. It was not just the time of day, but the season. The light was not that of a fresh spring morning or of a bright summer day. She found that it tapped into a deep longing for the sacred.

The second half of a woman's life offers some of the most complex and spiritually rich decades she will know. We are only beginning to fully recognize their challenge and promise. In this book I explore the spiritual dimensions of these middle and late years. In doing so I weave together two areas of personal experience and interest: the field of aging, and developments in women's spirituality.

Society is in the midst of an important aging trend, and the majority of older persons are women. Women over sixty-five are the fastest growing segment of the American population, and their average age continues to rise. By the end of this decade, there will be six women for every man over the age of eighty years in the more developed areas of the world. By 2010 nearly half of all adult women in America (aged twenty-one and older) will be at least fifty years old. Clearly, women are central to the story of aging in this century. However, as women age, we face the double stigma of being both old and female. The invisibility that results deprives our churches and communities of the rich, full experience of a large segment of the population at a time when pressing global issues require all the wisdom humanity can muster.

To change this negative view, we need an understanding of the realities and possibilities of the second half of women's lives. The interdis-

1

ciplinary resources of women's spirituality can help us discover and create these. Though not yet fully mined for insights on aging, women's spirituality offers us the tools of such discovery: a starting point and grounding in women's experience, a renewed sense of the power of the imagination, a focus on community and connectedness, increased awareness of our embeddedness in the rest of the natural world, the recovery of female symbols for the sacred, and of biblical and tradition-al stories of women. In relating these themes to the second half of women's lives, I draw primarily on the Christian streams of women's spirituality, but I also incorporate insights from other traditions where helpful.

While giving workshops and classes on spirituality and aging, I have learned how difficult it is to talk about an experience as diverse as aging. In our discussions we have veered back and forth, like someone just learning to ride a bicycle, between a consideration of the gifts of aging and a focus on its losses. Is it the best of times or the worst of times? An effort to stress the positive side of aging can mask its adver-sities. A focus on the problems of aging can obscure its possibilities. Finding God in the experience of aging requires a double vision, the paradox at the heart of the gospel. There we meet the paschal mystery, the intertwining of death and life. We are asked to somehow hold together the reality of suffering and loss with the truth of resurrection and new life. A woman described it in terms of the seasons. Her life felt like the autumn she was enjoying in nature in early October that year: "The days are gorgeous and full of color," she said, "but I know that it will be cold at night and get dark earlier. It is a very good time, but more lies behind than ahead. There is a poignancy and sadness along with the happiness."

The individual themes I explore throughout these chapters are drawn from women's experience as I have found it expressed in conversations, women's writing, and recent research. In developing these subjects I try to let women speak in their own words as often as possible. My hope is that this will help women of all ages, as well as women and men together, talk more fully about our spiritual experiences as we age. Although we are usually not interested in the geography of aging until we arrive within its borders, it shapes our vision of life and the choices we make in earlier years in important ways. Lack of awareness of its realities separates us from our future selves. We need to hear more of one another's stories if we are to live well all the seasons of the life cycle.

In the interests of such a dialogue, I begin with a discussion of how personal and societal images of older women constrict our sense of worth and our possibilities. I then suggest ways in which we can embrace new visions of ourselves. Next I explore the place in women's spirituality of transitions, an inner life, contemplation, the body, mourning, remembering, caregiving, and intergenerational connections. In treating these topics, I do not sharply distinguish between the middle and later years. Although many helpful insights have come from such demarcations, too often they simply prevent women from learning from one another's experience. I am struck more by what we share in common during these decades than by what divides us, and I try to describe aging as a process that has many individual variations.

Women frequently ask me for rituals and prayers to mark the passages of the second half of life. At the end of each chapter, I suggest some that I have developed. My intention is to offer ideas which can be creatively adapted or expanded.

I am grateful to have worked with many women as spiritual director, social worker, therapist, and teacher. I thank them as well as my family and friends for their many contributions to this book. The insights and stories they have shared with me are woven into this work; their identities have been concealed to preserve confidentiality.

Chapter 1

Visions of Ourselves

> We who are old know that age is more than a disability. It is an intense and varied experience, almost beyond our capacity at times, but something to be carried high.
>
> —Florida Scott-Maxwell, *The Measure of My Days*[1]

As women begin to tell their stories, we catch glimpses of what the middle and later years are like. No longer defined mainly by others, aging women emerge from the shadows as persons of strength and creativity, seasoned in suffering and love. Freed from the artificial sameness to which we were once reduced, we come now in many guises, with a mixture of human qualities. Some tell stories of a new freedom to contribute to family, church, and world. Others witness to poverty, lack of access to health care, and homelessness. Some are accounts of happiness and satisfaction; others, reports of bitterness and despair. Writers of fiction have begun to delineate a kind of freedom found by women as they age. Toni Morrison says of one of the central women characters in her novel, *The Song of Solomon*:

> Then she tackled the problem of trying to decide how she wanted to live and what was valuable to her. When am I happy and when am I sad and what is the difference? What do I need to know to stay alive? What is true in the world?[2]

One conviction guides this woman's efforts. Since death holds no terrors for her ("she spoke often to the dead"), she knows there is nothing to fear.

Stories of women's experience inspire and instruct us, but so far our sightings remain fleeting and partial. Women's own interpretations of aging are not yet available to any significant degree. Furthermore, as a woman ages, her voice is muted by what church and society say she is

...d can do. We must search for her through many disguises. Negative visions of her worth and potential limit a woman's sense of self and her possibilities. If women are to find the last half of life a time of psychological and spiritual growth, we must examine the power of these cultural images and recognize the unjust social policies they foster.

Concern for the full humanity of all persons is at the center of Jesus' message. Luke's gospel tells the story of a bent-over woman whom Jesus makes whole. Crippled for eighteen years, the woman cannot stand up straight. Jesus encounters her in one of the synagogues where he is teaching on the sabbath:

> When Jesus saw her he called her over and said, "Woman, you are rid of your infirmity" and he laid his hands on her. And at once she straightened up, and she glorified God (13:12–13).

Jesus decides to heal this woman on the sabbath, in a public house of prayer. His adversaries object, but he makes clear that persons are much more sacred than any customs or regulations. Though the officials seethe over Jesus' actions, the people rejoice.

This story delivers hope to all women convinced that they glorify God by standing tall in the fullness of their being. A contemporary woman poet reflects:

> A woman is bent.
> Surely You meant when You lifted her up
> long ago to Your praise, Compassionate One,
> not one woman only,
> but all women bent by unbending ways.[3]

Negative beliefs about women and aging are yokes impeding the expression of our gifts. Lifting these burdens and creating fresh visions of what it is to be an older woman is the starting point for a spirituality that will sustain us during the second half of our lives.

Images That Bind

Several years ago a woman from a religious congregation in the Southeast wrote to say that as she and others in her community approached retirement age, they were "defeating themselves daily in the imagination." "What I want," she said, "is some help to deal with imagination—to use it well, to channel it into green fields without trammeling it between rigid walls." She was right. The imagination is crucial to how we enter into the aging process; it constructs and mediates the world to us. The imagination reveals to us both our limits and the way to transcend them.

Older women, like old forests, are not highly valued by our society. The term itself has unpleasant connotations. Words like crone or hag, once titles of honor for a wise old woman, have become in common language vehicles for derision.

> My fantasy of old age or growing older was filled with fear, because it looked pretty awful to me. My fear was that I would become stupid, inept, helpless, and living in an old people's home alone and lonely. So I wanted to find models who could give me hope. I've found wonderful models and I've continued to look for new ones.[4]

Making older women unattractive is a way of convincing ourselves that we have nothing in common with them. As in all prejudice, we then live by a kind of oppositional thinking, creation of the not-I, the old woman. Older women become the "other." We project onto them the elements we do not want to claim in ourselves: vulnerability, mortality, uselessness, powerlessness. As repositories of qualities not integrated into our own self-image, they then become the antithesis against which we define ourselves.

These external depictions do not match our subjective experience as we age. Often we only realize that we have moved into the category of what society terms *old* when people begin to treat us differently. We are feeling good about ourselves, glad to be exactly where we are. Then someone addresses us in a patronizing tone as we stand in a supermarket line or arrive at a church gathering; suddenly we look in the mirror and decide that we do look different. Sara-Patton Boyle describes this experience in *The Desert Blooms: A Personal Adventure in Growing Old Creatively*. She terms it a case of mistaken identity:

> But people no longer saw me as me, a person like themselves. They saw me as an old woman, a stereotype composed of all the misconceptions and surrounded by the many conflicting feelings that the old-woman image inspires in our day.[5]

This discovery, she says, was numbing. Being related to as a category placed her outside the realm of human relationships.

Because aging is culturally defined in ways that do not correspond with our experience, we find it hard to call ourselves old. What we know of our lives and those of others strongly contradicts the socially constructed view of the older woman. Aging is too varied and intense an experience; arbitrary standards do not capture its complexity and depth:

> I want to cry out that the invisible part of me is not old. I still thrill to the beauties of this world—the dew upon the rose at dawn, the glow reflected by the sun on passing cloud when day is done.[6]

Age is somehow both distant and close at the same time, a stranger beginning to make herself at home. Our protests against being called old are rooted in the gap between stereotype and reality, in the pain of being shunted into categories that do not fit.

When women in mid-life tell me they are beginning to feel old, I ask what that means to them. They reply that they feel less energetic and attractive; they look in the mirror and see grey hair, facial wrinkles, sagging skin. Old equals loss of beauty. In *Faces of Women and Aging*, therapist Sarah Pearlman analyzes what she calls "late mid-life astonishment."[7] Many women between the ages of fifty and sixty, she says, suddenly become aware of the subtle changes that have been taking place in their appearance, recognizing with shock their diminished physical and sexual attractiveness. These physical changes, along with changes in health, can trigger a crisis in self-esteem; however, confronting them leads to new levels of self-confidence.

Accenting our losses, Pearlman stresses, is the stigmatization of aging with which women in particular must contend. Society convinces us that our value as women lies in *still* looking young, whatever our age. This makes the aging process very difficult, especially if a woman's identity has been tied to physical beauty. In *The Summer Before the Dark*, Doris Lessing's heroine, who suddenly experiences herself as middle-aged, feels "as if all her life she had been held aloft by the notice of other people as a flower is held up by water in its stamen, and now that water had been drained away."[8] Instead of being free to move with integrity into the next stages of our lives, we are caught up in a desperate and ultimately futile struggle to ignore or deny the reality of our own aging. We focus energy on maintaining as youthful an image as possible. Dependent on outside approval for a sense of worth, our value rises or falls with our sense of how well we are measuring up to an external norm of youthful beauty. The very real prejudice that exists when we do not meet this measure frightens and disheartens us.

Because looking like an older woman has negative consequences in the job market, the social realm, and every area of life, we try to pass for less than our age. A woman who was eighty-one described for me how she told everyone she was seventy-one; it was the only way she had any hope of getting a job, and she could not survive without some income. The diet, cosmetic, and cosmetic surgery industries have a large economic stake in keeping this focus on youthfulness alive. But a preoccupation with looking young draws energy away from a woman's inner life and diminishes her attention to other projects. It also divides women from one another. Once, when I was giving a conference on spirituality and aging, a woman in her sixties said she had hated to miss my session, but she did not want anyone to think she was old. The fear of aging severs the links between generations of women. Most seriously for all women, it truncates and distorts the meaning of the female life span.

If we are to offer society an alternative to communities that exclude, we need an ideal to enliven us. The gospel offers one. It presents a vision which runs counter to divisions based on such factors as gender and age. Honoring the unique gifts of persons at each stage of the life cycle brings us closer to this gospel ideal of community. Jesus preaches a God who is all-inclusive love, who lets the sun shine and the rain fall equally on all (Matt 5:45). This God of graciousness and goodness accepts everyone, bringing about justice and well-being for all without exception.[9] The parables tell us repeatedly of this inclusive love of God: the lost are found, the uninvited are invited, the last are first. God is like the shepherd searching for the lost sheep, like the woman searching for her lost silver coin. God's presence and power are revealed in the wholeness and well-being of everyone.

From this graciousness of God is born the inclusive community which Jesus proclaims:

> Go and tell John what you have seen and heard: the blind receive their sight, the lame walk, lepers are cleansed, and the deaf hear, the dead are raised up, the poor have the good news preached to them (Lk 7:22).

Everyone is invited to Jesus' banquet feasts. *No one* is excluded.

We need to take back the power to define what it means to be an aging woman. We do this not only for ourselves and younger women who are searching for mentors for their later years, but for the spiritual health of our churches and society. In what follows we will explore some ways to heal the images that bind us: redefining beauty, honoring diversity, creating more adequate models of human development, freeing women's creative potential, and reclaiming women's spiritual power.

Redefining Beauty

The Japanese have an adjective for the beauty of aging: *shibui*.[10] We have no comparable word in English to capture the distinctive character revealed with age. We find it in the contrast between young saplings and old trees in a forest. The shapes of young and mature trees are straight and symmetrical, often so similar that they are indistinguishable. Old trees, bearing the furrows and scars of centuries, have a unique beauty. There are no two alike. Many ecological differences between young and ancient forests result from these distinct tree configurations.

Human beauty can take startling forms. At present society defines it in terms of the body's conformity to set norms. However, the most compelling beauty emerges from the depth and texture of a person's life and spirit, and the face seems to carry it in a special way. Our intense response to such beauty stems from qualities that evoke pleasure, satisfaction, and wonder.

> The woman whose season of childbearing is complete changes hue like the autumn leaves. Her hair touched with silver, her skin marked with the lines of living, she is nonetheless full of beauty. Much joy may abide in this phase of life. Sad, indeed, that few women are prepared for the process of menopause; few understand what to expect, how to cope with it, or how to make the most of the glory of their autumns—fall can be spectacular.[11]

The later years correspond to the mythological figure of the Crone, the beauty of the dark moon. This beauty lies deep within the self; no longer external, it cannot be taken away.

We can contribute to how beauty is defined for us as older women. Since the media shape the popular imagination so powerfully, their portrayal of us must be challenged. Among us are artists, writers, politicians, those with power to create new public images. A writer states her personal view of it:

> I cannot think of a single human being whom I have ever cherished whose appeal to me was based on youthful cosmetic attractiveness alone. As a matter of fact, I often turn in a crowded city to stare at a face on which experience has written a pattern of celebration.[12]

As older women emerge from invisibility, their public presence will help heal our societal imagination, expanding it beyond narrow definitions. This can sometimes be done simply by the narrating of an actual life. For example, the story of Velma Edwards, who at seventy-three has dedicated herself to improving life in an impoverished Honduran village, upsets our equation of age with withdrawal from society. While teaching sewing and other skills in the village, she trudges through floods that block roads and destroy bridges, uses a toilet sometimes occupied by a snake and scorpions, and has expanded her skills so that she can add a carpentry class to her program.[13]

Though we need to change conditions outside the self as well as within if we are to thrive, there is need for caution as we address the media's image of aging. As populations age, older persons are becoming an important new market. This presents the risk that aging will once again be defined according to a consumer model, i.e., we can avoid the stigma of old age by participating in a consumer-driven society. We stand in danger of creating norms that demand a certain type of old age, one in which we take charge of life to the very end. According to this model, as we age we should remain healthy, sexually active, engaged, productive, and self-reliant. Those whose aging is less rosy, those who do not fit this new image, conclude that something is wrong with them. It allows us to ignore the conditions of those who are old and poor—the majority of whom are women.[14]

This caution applies to other efforts to combat ageism as well. Betty Friedan's *Fountain of Age* is an example.[15] Friedan does us all a service by offering images of vibrant older people to the large audience of her best-selling book. Friedan views age as an important and rewarding developmental stage of life in which we become more ourselves, braver, more thoughtful, more inward, and thus better prepared than at any other life stage to develop psychologically and spiritually. She is right in saying that we have no guidebooks that fully affirm the new strengths that are emerging in us as we age. Chiefly the bearer of good news, she describes old age as an evolution. But ultimately, Friedan finds aging unacceptable. She does not really confront the realities of poverty, loss, declining health, or death. Like consumer-driven images, this splits apart the negative and positive aspects of growing old: frailty and strength, growth and decline, hope and death. What we need, rather, is a dialectical view that embraces both the decline of aging and the hope for new life. Instead of denying the losses, we look to faith to transform their meaning.

Honoring Diversity

Stereotypes, including those of older women, are simplified and standardized images. They reduce differences to a set of categories. They also conceal the injustices present because of realities such as gender, class, and race. Therefore, an effective way to counter their power is to lift up and honor diversity.

This process begins with the recognition that chronological age is an imperfect measure of human energy and potential; we actually become more, not less, diverse as we age. We know from experience how very different from one another persons can be when they reach the age of forty, sixty, or eighty, yet chronological scales continue to be used as a determining factor in public policy and decision-making. Sylvia Heschel, pianist and widow of the Jewish thinker, Abraham Heschel, appeals for a change. Categories, she maintains, are for things, not human beings. They oblige us to evaluate ourselves in terms of what others think.

> Let us not categorize by groups, nor call them names, nor set up number of years as the guidelines. Let us liberate ourselves from the machinations of this age of mechanics.[16]

As we age, we ourselves internalize these messages and learn to use chronology as a reason to limit our choices. We tell ourselves: "I'm too old to do that." To do what? To learn to play the violin. To join the Peace Corps. To write poetry. To return to school for a degree. To fall in love again. To make new friends. To change careers. Age itself does not set these limits. Women in their sixth, seventh, and eighth decades are doing all of them.

Several decades ago, developmental psychologist Bernice Neugarten stressed the point that context, not chronology, is crucial for understanding variations in aging.[17] Two factors that dramatically change the context of aging are economics and health. Economic differences widen with age; for women they reflect a lifetime of inequities. Women not only live longer; they have more chronic health problems, are poorer, and are more likely than men to be living alone.[18] Inadequate health care for women earlier in life contributes to later problems, and a low income follows women into retirement.

These injustices are more pronounced for women of color. Older African-American women, for example, are the poorest of the poor. They have smaller incomes and higher rates of poverty than black men, white women or white men. Hispanic women have poverty rates about double those of white women.[19] Black women have historically held low-paying jobs—as housekeepers or cooks—with little or no retirement benefits. One such woman is EdieLeu Lane of Mound Bayou, Mississippi. Now seventy-nine, she worked as a young woman in the cotton fields and later in a cafeteria job: "Honey, you never made enough to save nothing, not a dime. We never did think about what you're going to do about tomorrow. Whatever we had we just took one day at a time."[20] The challenge of the future will be to create policies that genuinely empower and integrate all elder women into society.

Our images of older women broaden still more when we reach for a global perspective. We then see how aging is shaped by the realities of war, the struggle for liberation, and rapid social change. In this context we meet women such as Antonia, a member of the Mothers and Grandmothers of the Plaza de Mayo of Argentina.[21] During the military regime six members of her family disappeared—two sons, their pregnant wives, and two unborn children. Though she never saw her own grandchildren, she was made an honorary grandmother because of the love and life she gave to so many others. During what would have been the years of her menopause, Antonia was either in the streets facing the anger and hostility of the military, asking for the return of her six disappeared family members, or in the home of another victim's family, giving aid and comfort. She committed her life to working for justice for others.

Like war, cultural change affects women's aging. Monu, a woman in her late fifties with whom I visited in New Delhi, told me that she has "learned patience by the route of suffering." Having struggled for several years with rheumatoid arthritis, she wants to remain active in spite of it. She has continued to volunteer in a hospital for lepers, and, when we met, was planning a trip to Kathmandu, Nepal, to work for a year. Monu worries about the future of older people in India. They used to be provided for by members of their extended family. Now that is becoming problematic, she says, as families break up and members move to urban areas. She sees the elderly in the cities having trouble surviving. Monu says that her relationship with her own daughter is filled with a mixture of pride and regret. She is proud that she has become a leading folklorist of India, but she is sad that she will have no grandchildren since her daughter has decided not to marry.

As we attend to the stories of individual women, stereotypes dissolve. No longer seen through a lens that reduces their richness, these women's lives have fresh power to instruct and challenge.

Creating New Models of Human Development

Developmental psychologists such as Eric Erikson, Carl Jung, and Daniel Levinson have helped us create useful visions of aging by showing us that human growth does not end when we are children or young adults. Their theories of psychological development encompass the entire life span. During the past decade I have integrated into my own spirituality of aging depictions of life's middle and late stages as found in the works of Erikson and Jung. Helpful as these schemes have been for understanding aspects of aging, we have begun to sense their limitations. Dominant conceptions of the self and the life cycle fail fully to reflect women's experience; nor do they foster the interdependence that is integral to all of life.[22]

A key critique of existing developmental theories is that they envision the human person as evolving through ever increasing stages of separation and personal independence. Most theories of self are based on a Western ethic of individualism, what has been called a "Lone Ranger" mode of meeting challenges.[23] According to this model, we evolve through a series of crises in which we achieve a sequence of separations from others. Autonomy and independence, rather than intimacy and closeness, become the touchstones of maturity. Where intimacy is a value, it occurs after a person has achieved identity. When personhood is founded on independence and autonomy, whole groups—older people, women, racial and ethnic minorities, the poor—can be seen as less than fully human. Life development becomes a process toward a peak with an upward and downward slope on either side.[24] When human life is understood in terms of this peak/slope model, aging becomes a fall from independence and power, the downward side of the slope.

There are as yet few long-term studies of women's development in and through adulthood, though more are now appearing.[25] However, a helpful view of human interaction is being fostered by psychiatrist Jean Baker Miller and her colleagues at the Stone Center for Developmental Research and Services at Wellesley College.[26] Miller developed her theory as an older woman, and it shows promise for an interdependent and aging society. These researchers suggest that women's predilection for defining the self in interrelationship and through human connection provides a better social model than the typically individualistic one. Their theory does not focus on separation and independence as the goal of human growth. Rather, women are seen to move from attachment to continued connection. They live by relationship and care, and strive for the development of the total self in relationship with others. A more complex self emerges within more complex relationships.

Since woman's growth always occurs in the context of relationships, she experiences the goal of independence as isolating and lonely.[27] Her self-understanding leads to an alternative different from either dependence or independence, one in which both autonomy and mutuality are part of all human life. This goal is sometimes called relational autonomy, or relational freedom. The kind of world this creates celebrates the deeply interdependent quality of existence.

Such a focus on process, relationship, and interaction is supported by a new physics that emphasizes flow, waves, and interconnections rather than the static structure and discrete, bounded objects existing separately in the space of Newtonian physics. It is a theory less centered in the ego and more attuned to the ecology of nature, one that allows us to live in greater moral unity with the entire universe. Mystics as well as scientists describe this interdependence of all reality, the dance of all being.[28] In this pattern of exchange and transformation, true freedom of spirit is born. The dance of the universe teaches us that there is no private, isolated redemption. We do not pull ourselves up by our own bootstraps. Coming to terms with dependence is a way of acknowledging the truth of our existence and the design of creation. It is not a failure to reach maturity.

The gospel also calls us to understand dependence in a new way. In John 15:1–11 Jesus describes the Christian community in terms of a vine and its branches. The vine metaphor evokes a vision of mutuality and indwelling.[29] The verb "abide," which occurs ten times in this passage, means to remain; it suggests constancy of presence. The term abide is used for Jesus' relationship to God, Jesus' relationship to the community, and the community's relationship to Jesus. From these relationships of constancy and mutuality, the community finds possibilities for its own existence. As a portrait of what life in community can be, the metaphor of the vine stands in contrast to Western individualism. Each individual in the community will prosper only insofar as they are members of the whole. Each is a branch of an intertwining vine, and is fruitful only when abiding with others in Jesus' love.

This shift in models has special significance as we age. The literature on aging often equates health and maturity with independence and self-sufficiency. The individualism is sometimes subtle: we are to strive to continue living alone, capable of doing things for ourselves, freed from being a burden to others. Dependence carries negative connotations; we are to avoid it at all costs. Although it is possible for us to become too readily dependent as we age, in ways not ultimately helpful to us, more often we struggle to face our real dependencies. As long as we continue to locate the goal of maturity in independence, aging will be a torturous passage. Moreover, clinging to an elusive independence will limit the fullness of our lives.

Understanding dependence is pivotal to a new model of maturity as we age. We move, not from dependence to independence, but from the kind of dependence we knew as a child to a mature dependence characterized by mutual exchange, by reciprocal giving and receiving over time. A wheelchair-bound resident of a nursing home describes such interchange as the secret to her consistent good spirits:

> Friends. I've made a few good ones here. My brain, my mouth, and my heart still work, so I use them. Take the aide who dresses me in the morning—she's having a hard time of it in her life. I always get to hear the latest about her sons and her ex-husband. Sometimes I put my two cents in. Mostly, I just listen so she can get it off her chest. I've got all the time in the world, so she pours her heart out. She does extra things for me, like get me night-gowns with ties in the back instead of snaps. She likes to see that I'm comfortable, and I like to nudge her into making a better life for herself.[30]

As this woman knows, dependency is a process in which we receive from others, in which we count on others to help us cope physically or emotionally. It takes many forms in relationships and changes throughout the course of a lifetime. There may be times when we must rely totally on others for even the most basic of physical needs and the preservation of our personal dignity, times when we struggle to believe in our own worth and the capacity of others to continue caring for us. It is especially then, as individuals and as a society, that we need the vision of an interdependent universe, the vision of mutuality and constancy found in the gospel image of the vine and the branches.

Freeing Women's Creative Potential

The development of the autonomy pole of self-in-relation is also key as women age. Much of what we know of this is drawn from women's personal accounts rather than research studies. Margaret Boegeman, who teaches creative writing to older women, describes her students' lives of self-determination.

> One woman, now eighty, walks daily the two miles from home to our class and back, carrying only her backpack and two dimes, so she can "call someone if she has to." Headlines of rape and assault do not daunt her. After all, she has homesteaded the California desert; she has whitewater rafted on the Colorado River; she has driven the Alaskan highway in winter. She has left one husband because he drank; she has watched another one die. She has left a man she loved, at age seventy-two, because he was a gambler. Her eldest daughter she lost ten years ago to cancer. What has she left to fear? Confidently she walks the streets, attends college, writes, paints, imagines her future.[31]

This woman plans to live to ninety-four, Boegeman says, to welcome in the new millennium. Her student's openness to life, confidence in its goodness, and strengthening through experience has inspired Boegeman at several rough spots in her own life. Moreover, in teaching older women she has been privileged to see their enormous potential for growth and development not yet charted by any psychology.

What some studies do indicate is that women are more autonomous in later life than earlier in the life cycle. The relational skills and capacity for friendship built over a lifetime are strengths in aging, but freedom from traditional roles also creates space for greater personal freedom. Reflection on the life course of female creativity indicates that it may be easier for an older woman to integrate unconventional strivings. This calls for a shift in which a woman comes to understand how she has split off part of her creative self and viewed it as masculine. She can then reconcile it with her concept of womanhood.[32]

For most women these patterns are seen as a continuation and expansion of earlier modes. In her study of elderly Jewish members of the Aliyah Center in Venice, California, anthropologist Barbara Myerhoff reflects on how the women she met there seemed able to transform their roles and sense of self in original and satisfying ways. One of them, Sonya, remarks:

> You could say I'm not one hundred percent objective, but I am of the opinion that maybe things get better for old women and not so much for the men.[33]

The other women agree. In nearly all circumstances, Myerhoff observes, the older women are more capable, active, and authoritative. Most of the women were born and spent much of their childhoods in small Yiddish-speaking villages known as *shtetls*, located within the Pale of Settlement of Czarist Russia. The *shtetl* woman realized herself through others—children, men, support of the needy. Yet Myerhoff observes how the women at the Center had learned to flexibly adapt their roles in ways highly suited to old age. Along with the ideal social role they were expected to fulfill—submissive, retiring, patient, without ambitions or aspirations of their own—the *shtetl* women had developed what could almost be called an underground role, with possibilities they mined in later life. The older Center women thus had two *shtetl* roles available to them, not only the idealized woman dictated by tradition, but the improvised role developed in response to practical exigencies. Like their *shtetl* forebears, the old women at the Center emerged as "strikingly vigorous, resourceful, indomitable, often rude and brazen, anti-authoritarian, outspoken, and submissive to no one."[34] They were determined to survive well in spite of external pressures, to shape their lives and mold their worlds. They learned to live engaged and original lives, meeting the small and large challenges of growing old—such as living alone and with little money—with creativity and dedication. This creativity found expression in the way in which they set their own standards for measuring growth and achievement, sought new meaning in their lives, and provided themselves with possibilities to replace those that had been lost.

Research also suggests that aging may bring a loosening of male/

female dichotomies, allowing both women and men to embrace more fully all of the human qualities available to any person.[35] According to some studies, after a lifetime of concern with preserving relationships and being compliant to maintain them, older women become more assertive and willing to risk the loss of a relationship in order to follow their own priorities. In other words, they learn to balance the needs of self with those of others. This is seen as a creative vitality in women that flowers in mid-life and beyond. From this perspective, aging is a ripening, a coming to fruition.

Cross-cultural research also indicates that middle age and later can be a time of greater freedom and influence for women. For example, in *In Her Prime*, anthropologists Judith K. Brown and Virginia Kerns bring together essays on the lives of middle-aged women in twelve cultures.[36] They conclude that this is the time in which a woman enjoys her greatest power, status, and autonomy. This increase in power and status is gradual in some cultures; in others, there is a sharp break with earlier requirements for women's seclusion and deferential behavior. Many of the limitations that surround younger women are removed in middle age. Also, restrictions on women's behavior stemming from the powers of menstrual blood or fertility are ended or diminished. At middle age women also gain social and economic authority, and they are able to aspire to positions that are age- or gender-related, such as those of midwife, political mediator, or ritual leader. In these cultures middle age is a woman's prime.

The authors note that these findings contrast with middle-aged women in our own society, where a valued status for older women does not exist. However, women in Western societies also describe themselves at different points along the path of aging as feeling as though they have come into their own. One woman said that both her grandmother and an older friend "really came alive" after the period of mourning following widowhood. This positive assessment is supported by research on widows' lives after they have worked through the shock and confusion of the loss.[37] For some women, this sense of fullness comes at a particular age. Carolyn Heilbrun writes in *Reinventing Womanhood*:

> I was in my fiftieth year when I began this book: for me a time of flowering. A friend wrote to me at Cambridge, after we had dined in New York: "You are in your prime." Women seldom think of themselves as in their prime at fifty, but I think it is often so.[38]

Others have told me this experience of fullness came at seventy or eighty. The timing seems to depend on a woman's inner and outer circumstances.

Clearly there is much yet to be learned in this area of personhood and human development across the life cycle. As more research becomes available to us, it both raises questions and challenges conventional answers. While middle and late age offer women greater possibilities, failure to realize their potential leads to problems both for women and for the societies of which they are a part. The creative vitality of women in the second half of life can be either recognized or denied by a culture. We are realizing how important it is that our own society begin more fully to honor it.

Reclaiming Women's Spiritual Power

Although poverty and illness can endanger the quality of our later years, we know that economic security and good health do not guarantee happiness. In counseling women who have reached their sixth and seventh decades, I hear a recurring theme. They and their husbands have retired. At first they looked forward to a life of playing golf and tennis, having lunch with friends, traveling. This wore thin in a short time. It did not answer their longing for purpose. They enjoy their children, but they realize that they have lives of their own and cannot supply meaning for them. Other women are single, divorced or widowed, and are looking for ways to combine the use of their gifts with the discovery of community. Still others are retired members of religious congregations. They are accustomed to having more satisfying outlets for their energy. They also have deep concern for the state of the world and a desire to live their Christian faith fully. They need useful channels for their talents.

Traditional societies have honored the older woman's spiritual power. She has been midwife, herbalist, healer, and teacher—the Wise Woman. Using insight honed by experience, she is advisor, judge, and arbiter. As crone, she is holy fury and knowledge, active wisdom. Close to life's cycles, she is leader of ceremonies for every event from birth to death.[39] Where the elder woman is feared and rejected, these functions are denied her.

Contemporary women are looking for ways in which this archetype might come to life in their times. We desire the freedom to explore unknown worlds within and without.

I look forward to the crone. I think that's the great gift that is the balancing force for all the things we give up by aging. What we get in return is the Wise Woman. I'm looking forward to her.[40]

The arrival of the wise woman means acknowledging the assets women have for a healthy, satisfying old age, and allowing these gifts to extend to all the spheres where they are needed. It means encouraging them to bring their talents to fruition in the world. It means honoring the anger that is seeking justice. Most important, it means affirming the spiritual power of women.

An intriguing biblical woman draws our attention as we reflect on this spiritual power. She appears in the early part of Luke's narrative: Anna, Phanuel's daughter, of the tribe of Asher (2:36–38). Her husband died after seven years of marriage, and the gospel tells us that she is now of great age, eighty-four (sixty years was considered old), and spends her time in the temple worshiping with fasting and prayer night and day. The reference to Anna takes up a very short space in the narrative, but in spite of her near invisibility there are three important things it tells us.

First, she is a widow and therefore belongs to a group of women mentioned a number of times in the New Testament. The widow is, like the stranger, the orphan, and the poor, a special object of God's concern. Jesus' treatment of these groups shows him to be a true advocate of the oppressed and exploited. In the story of the widow's mite, for example, we are asked to ponder the inner richness of the widow's life, in spite of her outer poverty. The widow's action is contrasted with those who give more, but are inwardly empty. She becomes a symbol of the way in which ordinary values are turned around in the reign of God brought by Jesus (Mk 12:41–44).

As a widow, Anna serves as a prototype for what later became an order of consecrated widows and for the place of widows in general in the church's earliest periods. The community was asked not only to respond to the needs of widows, but to encourage their contributions as well. It is clear that a large and active office for older women existed in the church.[41]

A second thing to note about Anna is that she is the first evangelist. At the end of the gospels, women proclaim the resurrection. Here, at the beginning, we find an older woman proclaiming Jesus' advent. When she sees the child with his mother, Anna heralds Jesus "to all who were looking for the redemption of Jerusalem" (Lk 2:38).

Finally, Luke presents Anna to us as a prophetess. She stands in the tradition of Miriam, Deborah, and Huldah, and foreshadows the other women who receive this calling, among them, the daughters of Philip (Acts 21:9). As a prophetess, Anna is a woman divinely inspired to make known God's word to others. She is able to see and interpret for her people the hidden revelation of God, the meaning of the events of their time and the call to turn to the ways of God. Anna witnesses to the coming of the day of the Lord: "I will pour out my Spirit on all people. Your sons and daughters will prophesy" (Joel 2:28; Acts 2). The story of Anna can serve to underscore the spiritual potential of older women. Poised at the end of one era and the beginning of another, she is rooted in the ways of God and able to point her people to a future of trust and promise.

The Native American tradition also contains many stories of women's spiritual paths. The last of these is the way of the wise woman. It is that period of a woman's life when she has reached the fullness of her age. Now entering her period of mastery, the shaman, or wise woman, has developed true wisdom. Her balance and sense of humor are at its peak. Her vocation is that of furthering the well-being of the planet and the cosmos.

> The sphere of her work has broadened far beyond that of her personal, private self and of her familiar group; her community extends to the stars.[42]

The wise woman has learned to walk in the ways of beauty, balance, and spiritual power. She is now complete, having walked the Sacred Hoop, the medicine wheel of life.

This vision, so compelling in its rich presentation of the older woman as wise woman, comes from a tradition in which relationships among all beings of the universe must be fulfilled if each individual life is to be fulfilled. In these traditions the sacred is imaged as the Old Woman who tends the fires of life, as the Old Woman Spider who weaves the fabric of interconnectedness. A Keres Indian song says:

> I add my breath to your breath
> That our days may be long on the Earth
> That the days of our people may be long
> That we may be one person
> That we may finish our roads together
> May our mothers bless you with life
> May our Life Paths be fulfilled.[43]

Here are promising seeds of a new image of the older woman. They plant in our imaginations a vision of ourselves as wise women whose roots are in the spiritual, whose personal outreach embraces the universe itself.

FOR PRAYER AND REFLECTION

1. Litany in Praise of Older Women

All: Divine Fountain of Life, we remember today all those older women who have revealed to us the gifts of age. Throughout time they have creatively brought hope and healing to our world. We call on these foremothers to help us discover your paths for our own lives.

We remember SARAH, keeper of the covenant and hope of her people, who linked generations with strands of laughter.
All: We ask for her gifts of candor and fidelity.

We remember NAOMI, mother-in-law and widowed foreigner, who found loyalty and fruitfulness in the midst of emptiness and exile.
All: We pray to find these harvests in our own emptiness.

We remember ANNA, widow and prophetess, who out of silence and prayer pointed us to the presence of the Holy in our midst.
All: We ask for her gifts of prayer and vision.

We remember ELIZABETH, wife of Zechariah and mother of John, who in old age kept faith with her own future while confirming the promises offered to her younger friend, Mary.
All: We ask for her readiness to share sacred stories.

We remember HILDEGARD OF BINGEN, twelfth-century scientist, poet, and mystic, who alerted us to the Divine Breath in clouds that billow, breezes that blow, and streams that nurture all things green.
All: We pray to know that we are one with all the earth.

We remember TERESA OF AVILA, sixteenth-century theologian and reformer, who in the second half of her life not only created a new religious order, but wrote a great mystical treatise.
All: We pray to realize our own life possibilities.

We remember all those wise women, herbalists and midwives, who were tried and executed as witches because of the fear and envy of their spiritual and healing powers.
All: We pray to recognize our own gifts of healing.

We remember SUSAN B. ANTHONY, advocate of women's liberation and steadfast reformer, who fought for women's right to vote.
All: We pray for her faith in women's potential.

We remember SOJOURNER TRUTH, abolitionist and advocate of women's rights, who promised that at her death she would go home like a shooting star.
All: We ask for her confidence in God's loving-kindness.

We remember MOTHER JONES, who lived to be a hundred striving for the dignity of the worker and the growth of the labor movement.
All: We pray for her concern for human dignity.

We remember ME KATILILI, Kenyan organizer and liberator, who at the age of seventy led the Giriama tribe's movement for freedom from British rule.
All: We pray for her commitment to human liberation.

We remember DOROTHY DAY, founder of the Catholic Worker Movement and social reformer, whose houses of hospitality continue to welcome the poor.
All: We pray for her belief in love as the measure of a life.

We remember the mothers and grandmothers of Argentina, fearless in their determination, who have kept vigil for their children and other loved ones tortured and disappeared.
All: We ask for their constancy in the face of evil.

We remember DOLORES HUERTA, vice-president of the United Farmworkers Union, who has been called *la pasionaria de Delano* in light of her commitment to the struggle of her people.
All: We pray for her faith in all people.

We remember ADELE O'SHAUGHNESSEY, long-time Pax Christi member and promoter of peace, who encouraged the young with her firm belief that peace is not only possible, but inevitable, if we all unite on behalf of our planet.
All: We pray for her commitment to peace in our world.

We remember TISH SUMMERS and LAURIE SHIELDS, founders of the Older Women's League which, with its motto, "Organize, don't agonize!" has worked vigorously for the rights of older women.
All: We pray for their dedication to women in need.

We remember MAGGIE KUHN, founder of the Gray Panthers, filled with rage and creativity into her eighties, who has worked against divisions between young and old in the struggle to end oppression.
All: We pray for her imagination and passion.

We remember THEA BOWMAN, singer of melodies of life, faith, and love, who showed us how to find joy even in the midst of illness and pain.

All: We pray for her heritage of optimism and song.

We remember our own mothers, and grandmothers, who by their love and their lives have taught us what it means to live and die as women.

All: We pray for the fullness of their gifts.

Let us remember any other women to whom we owe a debt of gratitude.

All: (Add any women you wish to remember or for whom you wish to pray.)

Let us remember older women everywhere, of every class, culture, race, and religion, as well as those who are in our midst today.

All: We pray they may know they are cherished by God, and use their gifts to the full.

Leader: (Closing Prayer—Based on Hildegard of Bingen)

> You bless with the Breath of Wisdom.
> Thus all of our praise is yours,
> You who are the melody itself of praise,
> the joy of life, the mighty honor,
> the hope of those to whom you give
> the gifts of the Light. Amen.[44]

2. Jubilee Year: A Fiftieth Birthday Ritual

Opening Song

Reading: "You are to count seven weeks of years—seven times seven years, that is to say a period of seven weeks of years, forty-nine years.

You will declare this fiftieth year sacred and proclaim the liberation of the inhabitants of the land" (Lev 25:8, 10).

Call to Gather: We join with our friend today to celebrate her year of Jubilee, her fiftieth birthday. The Jubilee is a time of restoration and renewal, of righting relationships with ourselves, God, and all creation. Our friend will renew her covenant with each of these.

I. The Covenant with Self:

Reading: (read by woman celebrating her Jubilee)

> Moon, wisp of opal fire, then slowly
> revealed as orb arising,
> still half-hidden; the dark
> bulk of the wooded ridge defined
> by serrations of pine and fir against
> this glow
>   that begins to change
> from lambent red to a golden
> pervasive mist of light as the whole
> fullness of moon
> floats clear of the hill.[45]

Restoration of Her Life: Each of those present tells an anecdote or story from the woman's life and, as she does, gives her a bead to be woven together and worn, or a piece of fruit for a basket.

Blessing (All lift hands or lay hands on her to bless her.)
We bless the hidden and visible light of your life. May you find the courage and hope to let the fullness of your moon arise.

II. The Covenant with God

Opening Words of Praise (prayed by the woman whose celebration it is)

> Blessed is She who spoke and the world became.
>   Blessed is She.
> Blessed is She who in the beginning, gave birth.
> Blessed is She who says and performs.
> Blessed is She who declares and fulfills.
> Blessed is She whose womb covers the earth.
> Blessed is She whose womb protects all creatures.
> Blessed is She who nourished those who are in awe of Her.
> Blessed is She who lives forever, and exists eternally.
> Blessed is She who redeems and saves. Blessed is Her Name.[46]

Silent Prayer: The woman celebrating and all present gather any prayers of praise, gratitude, regret, and petition that are in their hearts.

Sharing of Prayers: Those who wish, give voice to their prayers.

III. The Covenant with All Creation

Lament for Broken Relationships *(Recited Antiphonally)*

> Gaia, Mother Earth, we hear your pain and suffering,
>   your struggles for breath and life.
> We mourn our careless and heavy footsteps on your body.
>
> All oppressed peoples of the earth, we taste your hunger and
>   thirst for justice.
> We confess our failures to work for freedom and justice.
>
> Friends and family near and far, we see you reaching for
>   understanding and healing.
> We regret our actions and inactions, large and small, that
>   have brought you sorrow.

Renewal of Commitment: The woman celebrating her Jubilee describes the ways in which she wants her next decades to honor her bonds with all of creation and its peoples.

Reading: For I am about to create new heavens and a new earth; the former things shall not be remembered or come to mind. But be glad and rejoice forever in what I am creating, for I am about to create Jerusalem as a joy and its people as a delight....No more shall the sound of weeping be heard in it or the cry of distress.

No more shall there be in it an infant that lives but a few days, or an old person who does not live out a lifetime....They shall build houses and inhabit them, they shall plant vineyards and eat their fruit. They shall not build and another inhabit; they shall not plant and another eat; for like the days of a tree shall the days of my people be.

Before they call I will answer, while they are yet speaking I will hear. The wolf and the lamb shall feed together, the lion shall eat straw like the ox. But the serpent—its food shall be dust. They shall not hurt or destroy on all my holy mountain, says the Lord (Is 65:17–22, 24–25).

Refreshments and Dancing

Chapter 2

Grace in Transitions

The autumn of a woman's life is far richer than the spring if only she becomes aware in time and harvests the ripening fruit before it falls and rots and is trampled underfoot. The winter that follows is not barren if the harvest has been stored, and the withdrawal of sap is only the prelude to a new spring elsewhere.

—Irene Claremont de Castillejo, *Knowing Woman*[1]

A colleague had just celebrated her fiftieth birthday and was returning home with a friend and her daughter. With them was the daughter's young playmate. The girls' conversation in the back seat included the following question from the youngest: "How does it feel to be five? Is it different from being three?"

Aging is a process of growth that begins with birth and continues throughout life. Like this young girl, we want to know what the next stage will be like, and we look for clues from those who have been there. We anticipate the rewards of being five, or sixteen, or twenty-one. Change is at the heart of aging. At some point, however, a shift occurs. Change no longer holds appeal and promise: "Fifty was a hard birthday," a woman told me, "I'm beginning to feel old. I figure I have about twenty good years left. Then ten marginal ones. Then it's downhill after eighty. Suddenly I feel the shortness of time." Change now looms like a thief ready to rob us of valued possessions. Yet how we respond to it determines everything.

Aging is a mosaic of transitions or passages.[2] Some of these are under our control. We choose to move to another city, to start a new career, to retire. Other changes are thrust upon us: our husband leaves us for another woman; we experience the signs of menopause; we develop arthritis and cannot walk as well as before; a partner, parent, or friend dies. Some passages are marked by outer events like the birth of a grandchild; others are shifts in meaning and value invisible to the outer eye. Transitions do not always arrive singly; we may be moving through several at once. Today, transitions are made more difficult for women by the fact that we have few role models. Not many women at the beginning of the century lived to experience the decades we now face; their roles lasted for as long as they lived, which was about forty-eight. We are in uncharted territory.

Whether chosen or imposed, inner or outer, transitions are not only psychological and social events, but religious passages. God is always found within, not apart from, ordinary human experience. The gospels often use images from daily life to describe the divine in us: seeds disintegrating in the dark earth and sprouting fresh and green; fields of rippling grain ripe and ready to be harvested; lovers and laborers, daughters and sons, being accepted and forgiven in ways beyond their wildest expectations. The parables convey the core of Jesus' teaching, that the realm of grace is the ordinary.

All transitions follow a similar cycle. The process takes us from ending and relinquishment, through emptiness and darkness, to fresh life and new beginnings. This movement reminds us of the cyclical nature of all of life: the pattern of the seasons, the waxing and waning of the moon, the ebb and flow of the tides. Progress is not always swift and straight. There is compensation, adjustment, and circling back.[3] Our adult lives include many cycles of stability followed by periods of transition. For change is not simply a moment of our existence, but its pattern.

Faith tells us that this circle of loss and gain is a crucible of transformation. It is the paradox of the gospel: If you want to keep your life, give it away. A seed must die to bring forth fruit. During the immense struggle to embrace loss and change what we most need is hope, the trust that if we loosen our grip on the old, we will still have something. Part of this hope is being able to understand in faith the pattern of transitions: the ending, the period in-between, and the emergence of something new. Each stage has its characteristic challenges and graces.

The Sense of An Ending

The endings that lead to transformation are essential to the process; there can be no rebirth without a death. Some part of us believes this. Yet it is natural to cling to the familiar and fear the unknown. We grieve for our youth, for our strong bodies, for the sense that we were needed, for the tattered dreams and ideals that we see no way of mending. Often when we feel we cannot bear another ending, it is pressed upon our lives anyway: a parent's sickness, the death of a friend, a diagnosis of illness. We may be dealing not simply with one major transition, but with many small or large ones. Even when the event is one we welcome or find relatively easy—as some women do with menopause, retirement, or the leaving home of children—it still involves adjustment. At menopause, for example, our bodies signal the end of our reproductive phase and we begin to learn a new way of thinking and feeling, a way of being in the world and contributing to it that is no longer tied to the possibility of creating children. For some women these changes may take place below the threshold of awareness, preoccupied as they are with other things in their lives. There is much diversity in our transitions.

Transitions often find us unprepared. For example, a sister writes about the experience of aging members of religious orders. Many older religious, in that stage of life now often referred to as the Third Age, simply drift into this phase of their lives, she says. They did not prepare for retirement and leisure and are not automatically ready to embrace a deeper spirituality.

> The same obstacles to prayer and reflection faced during the Second Age remain. The aging religious should not be expected to gratefully embrace a new life of prayer and contemplation when they have spent so much of their lives absorbed in their work.[4]

She believes that for many religious a sense of self is tied to what one does rather than who one is, and they suffer a diminishment of ego strength when they can no longer work.

Change is difficult. One of the hardest struggles comes when we sense that something is ending and it is time to let go. This sense of an ending may arrive in an intuitive, internal shift. We begin to notice our mortality. Old motivations and enthusiasms seem inadequate. We are indifferent to things that once stirred us. Our focus starts to shift.

> Dreams come. Memories present themselves. As sure as birth contractions come to separate us from the safety of the womb, some hidden timing stirs us, bringing a sense of readiness for the new. We wake one morning to find that we are no longer able to squeeze into our old identity.[5]

Significant passages do not wait for our permission, and they ignore our illusion that change and death are no part of our lives. We begin a period of self-questioning and self-revelation. We examine our relationships with children, parents, spouse, community, friends, and our own inner self. Transitions take us through a continuous process of losing and finding a new identity. We are no longer the same person after important life changes, and we have to bid farewell to one sense of self without knowing what we will be like in the future.

Whether the ending is inner or outer, the language of letting go is dominant as women describe the initial stage of a transition. A daughter says of her ninety-year-old mother that one of the things she is teaching her is how to let go. A friend in her fifties describes an experience she has: "From time to time I will awaken with a sentence, almost like a whisper: 'Let go.' 'Let go of what?' 'Just let go.'" Another woman expresses her sense of it this way: "There is something like surrender involved in all of this. But not in a passive way. It is very intentional and active." What women name as letting go is not simply resignation to the inevitable; it is a deep inner shift, often the outcome of a process of resistance and struggle.

Two gifts of the Spirit are key to this phase of a transition: discernment and simplicity. What does God want of me? Many areas call out for attention. Discernment is a way of listening both to our deepest selves and to outer events, so we can come closer to God's vision for our lives. We need the gift of discernment because it is not always clear when to let go and when to hang on, whether acceptance or defiance is the best path in a particular situation. This is especially true for us as women. The timing of transitions reflects cultural expectations and norms. Age and gender can be major, and often unjust, ways of determining roles in a society. A woman's life course is also more complex than a man's due to these expectations. Because of earlier mothering responsibilities, some women are just entering the strongest point of their careers or finding a professional direction when men are ready to retire. A woman who enters college when she is eighty goes against accepted norms. Her refusal to retire when she feels capable and loves her job challenges assumptions about age and work. A woman who enjoys developing her talents as an artist more than caring for her grandchildren evokes judgment. An older woman who insists that she has key contributions to make in the public arena defies cultural roles. Women want to be there for those who need them, but as they age they also want to take more time for themselves, enjoy the present, and select their own priorities.[6]

Discernment is also needed with regard to the physical limitations that come with age. A friend with a progressive neurological disease ponders the question often: "How hard do I push myself? Should I just give in and take it easier?" I also remember a woman I met when I first started working in a nursing center. She had been through a severe stroke and was with us to recover. There was every reason to believe that she would never return home. A woman of deep faith, she agonized with me over the choices. Should she bend to events and give up her desire to be back in her house, or pour all her energy into making it back? I was cautious about her chances, but she chose the latter path and proved me wrong. She lived at home for several more years. Later, she had a second stroke and returned to the nursing center. "I can't do it again," she said. "This time I must find a way to be happy here. Deep down inside me something has shifted, and I know I am on a different path."

Along with discernment, this phase of a transition calls for the simplifying of our lives. Simplicity is a creative response to the awareness of limits. Times of transition force us to trim away the nonessential. The novelist Isabel Allende explains this shift after turning fifty: "I don't have any time to waste. I don't have time for gossip or greed or revenge or undirected anger."[7] She says she is concentrating on the basics, which have to do with love. This same theme appears in May Sarton's novel, *A Reckoning*. When Laura Spelman learns that she has inoperable cancer, her one wish is to be allowed to die in her own way, with as little medical intervention as possible. For her, this last illness is a journey during which she must come to a final reckoning with everything:

> When I was told what the matter was, all that day I kept thinking that now I could plan my life, maybe for the first time, and the phrase that kept coming back was "the real connections." I did not need to have anything to do with what was not a real connection.[8]

Laura finds that setting a limit gives her an enormous sense of relief and freedom; she no longer has to try so hard. Cutting out the nonessential leaves time simply to be—to watch the light on the wall, play music, read the things she wants to read.

As we age, it may feel as though we are shrinking. After a lifetime of collecting and saving, our belongings are too much for us. The house we live in feels too large. We have a deep inner urge to simplify. The British travel writer Freya Stark writes in *The Journey's Echo*:

> In our increasing poverty, the universal riches grow more apparent, the careless showering of gifts regardless of return; our private grasp lessens, and leaves us heirs to infinite loves in a common world where every joy is a part of one's personal joy. With a loosening hold returning towards acceptance, we prepare in the anteroom for a darkness where even this last personal flicker fades, and what happens will be in the Giver's hand alone.[9]

Though at first not fully conscious, a sorting and scaling down has begun. "Take nothing for the journey," Jesus says. "Sell all you have and give to the poor." The gospel parable about the treasure hidden in a field fits this mood. We sell what we have to find that treasure. We discover our true keepsakes: the sound of wind moving through the grass, the light glancing off water, the lingering melody of a favorite song, the bubbling laughter of a child, the love of a friend.

This desire to find the one thing necessary illumines a spontaneous ritual that often arises during the passage into the later decades. Women give away things. When my mother picked out and offered me a dish she had received at her engagement party some sixty years earlier, I wept on the way home. She had said only: "Choose the one you would like." But the gift also said: "I don't need these things any more. I want you to have something of mine that I treasure. I am getting ready to go." Our many transitions prepare us for the final passage through death into risen life.

The Time In-between

Making a transition is like entering another country. At the border we stand between receding landscapes and as yet unexplored territory. It is a spaceless, undefined place, sometimes called "a neutral zone."[10] One woman calls this period "supervising the chaos."

As we enter the middle and later years, the things that gave our lives meaning begin to drop away. A woman in her forties reflects:

> I know the idea of a midlife crisis has been trivialized, but I really am at that point where I'm asking, "What's the meaning?" I try to answer this question with my job and my marriage, but it doesn't

work. Everything feels like a *should*—even to the point where I
should save the world. I can't embrace anything with joy.

The darkness that ensues does not feel rich with gifts; it is instead a
frightening void. We had expected more from life. This search for
meaning is the core of the later decades. We may previously have filled
the emptiness; now we must stay with it as it leads us into the unknown.
A woman imaged this by saying that she wanted to be in meditation
with a shawl wrapped around her, waiting for rebirth. How long we
stay in this place of waiting and uncertainty depends on many things,
including our economic, social, and family situation and our individual
rhythm.

During the weeks when a friend in her eighties was preparing to
move to a retirement complex, she found herself suspended between
the home she had known and a strange new living place.

> The hardest part is the darkness and emptiness. I've been through
> this many times, but this is the worst it's been. I'm still walking
> with the Lord as my constant companion, but I'm losing myself,
> my creativity, my inner resources. I always had that to draw on
> before. For the past year, when I go to bed at night, I pray that I
> won't wake up in the morning.

In our conversations, my friend told me how she made it through this
period. Like flowers and roots in the desert that cling to water and hoard
their moisture, she held onto the smallest glimmers of hope offered her
by friends and family. Reassurance and support from friends made all
the difference. As Adrienne Rich says of birth in *Of Woman Born*, when
a woman is in labor, she may turn to a midwife and say: "Do something! I can't go on! Help me!" What she is asking in this time of transition is: "Assist me. Support me. Tell me this is supposed to happen."[11]

Faith illumines this fallow period when something new is being
born. We turn for insight to the gospel resurrection narratives. Women
are prominent in these stories, suspended between the mysteries of
death and new life. All four gospels agree on one important detail about
Easter morning: the women went to Jesus' tomb in the early morning
hours, while it was still dark. Their faithfulness is apparent even in this
time of darkness.

One of the stories about women at Jesus' tomb is of Mary Magdalene
(Jn 20:1–18). She is the first witness of the empty tomb. When she

arrives, she sees that the stone has been rolled away. She runs and reports this to Peter and the beloved disciple, offering what appears to be the only logical explanation of the fact—someone has stolen the body. Mary's confusion reflects the way in which the empty tomb shatters all previous ways of seeing things. There are no categories to explain it. No words from previous experiences adequately describe it. In our own times of emptiness we identify with this shattering of expectations and loss of categories of explanation.

We find the same themes in another familiar Easter story. We walk for a moment with the two disciples on the road to Emmaus (Lk 24:13–35). It is springtime in Jerusalem, and the city is bustling with pilgrims. This festive mood contrasts with the somber faces and heavy hearts of the two who are making their way the seven miles from Jerusalem to Emmaus. They are experiencing loss and uncertainty, caught in the empty space between Good Friday and Easter Sunday when something has ended and nothing has yet taken its place. Jesus joins the two, but they do not recognize him. They reveal the reason for their downcast spirits: "Our own hope had been that he would be the one to set Israel free." Their expectations have been dashed. Their plans lie in ruins. Then Jesus begins to talk with them, showing them that they must live without certain expectations if new hope is to be born.

This period between Good Friday and Easter Sunday feels as if it will last forever. The loneliness is hard, and we wish for escape. A woman without a job and low on money says:

> It's difficult to cope with the uncertainty of how long this "in-between" time will last—until next week, next month, next Christmas?...I keep praying to know what I can learn from this time.

Another woman searches for a God who seems absent in her life:

> O God, where have you been? You were so important in my twenties. Will you come back? How?

A mother describes the experience of having the last of her three sons leave home:

> I don't know if I will ever get over it. I may always feel this mourning.

Our ties to the familiar are severed and we are at a loss. It is a time of chaos and uncertainty, but also a time for trust. It takes trust to wait, to believe in the rhythm of an emerging process. If the temptation of the first phase of a transition, the ending, is to refuse to let go when it is time, the temptation of this phase is to fill the emptiness with anything we can. We might do this by getting too busy, by trying to reinstate the old, by settling for a quick solution: "I keep wanting to fill it up right away. This waiting is so hard." Just as a butterfly cannot be forced from its cocoon before it is time, so we must trust that during this fallow period our knowledge and desires are being transformed. Though this in-between period is a time of activity—gathering information, talking with friends, seeking support, considering options—it is also a time of waiting for the answer being formed within. Foundational decisions are given to us as much as they are shaped by us. Fallow time allows space for the work of our creative and imaginative selves. These powers work slowly and quietly, at a deep level of the self, and as we listen to that place, we begin to know what we must do. Often we are aware that clarity has been reached when we begin to tell others what we intend to do.

Two gifts of the Spirit bring us through in-between times: courage and hope. Courage carries us across challenging terrain to a place we cannot yet envision. Like a bridge spanning churning waters, it supports us during the passage. It is impossible fully to know the outcome of a process before it is complete; we are fearful and uncertain. Will I really be able to change careers and survive? Will I find something to fill my life now that my former sense of meaning has vanished? If I relinquish my image of the ideal marriage, what will take its place? Walking with women in transition, I hear these cries of the spirit: Who will I be? What will I do? What will others think?

Courage evokes images of large, heroic deeds. But it dwells as often in the midst of ordinary routine, in the details of love as well as in its grand schemes. In her poem, "Courage," Anne Sexton charts its presence in the small events of our lives: a child's first step, learning to ride a bike, being called names and not letting others know it hurts, enduring a great despair alone. She concludes:

> Later,
> when you face old age and its natural conclusion
> your courage will still be shown in the little ways,
> each spring will be a sword you'll sharpen,
> those you love will live in a fever of love,

> and you'll bargain with the calendar
> and at the last moment
> when death opens the back door
> you'll put on your carpet slippers
> and stride out.[12]

Courage is what enables us to let go, to live in the darkness, to begin again. It gives us the strength to risk.

Courage is not a quality of the solitary self. It is created and sustained in community. Even when alone, we draw on others to strengthen us. Courage is born in the experience of being loved and upheld. It is rooted in grace. For women, transitions threaten the loss of connection; hope depends on new relationships. Sitting with a woman in her fifties who had just begun a new job, I asked her what was hardest about this frightening time in her life. She described how alone and disconnected she felt at meetings and workshops. No one knew or related to her in terms of who she was. Another woman struggling with depression in her seventies said it seemed to her that other women were joined in groups, and she was not. She pictured herself as standing alone on the outskirts of these communities. On the other hand, a church group offered the strongest support for a woman whose husband had asked for a separation after forty years of marriage. The church provided the structure and space for the women to meet in informal ways—for a potluck, a picnic, discussions. Here she came to know other women whose experiences were like her own, women who had survived and were thriving. It gave her confidence that she could do the same.

In addition to courage, we need hope. Like courage, hope is always somehow an act of community. It may be as small as two people helping one another survive a tragedy or as large as the global community searching for a way to save our planet. Though we tend to think of hope as arising in isolation, as the achievement of individuals, the truth is that we develop it in one another. How do we do this? We lose a job or receive a diagnosis of breast cancer. Someone listens to us, offers us encouragement, suggests a path—and the hope that was extinguished flickers again. A friend or family member dies, and we are plunged into grief and mourning. Friends stay with us through the darkness; one day new energy stirs within us. We wonder if we have anything left to contribute, whether our gifts really matter. Then we read of others who believe that even small deeds make a difference. Their witness restores to us a sense of the possible. Their deeds are strands of hope pulling us forward. In her poem, "For the New Year, 1981," Denise Levertov speaks of such shared hope as small grains or crystals of grace. We need more than we have.

> I break off a fragment
> to send you.
>
> Please take
> this grain of a grain of hope
> so that mine won't shrink.
>
> Please share your fragment
> so that yours will grow.
>
> Only so, by division,
> will hope increase,
>
> like a clump of irises, which will cease to flower
> unless you distribute
> the clustered roots, unlikely source—
> clumsy and earth-covered—
> of grace.[13]

Grains and crystals of hope. These are the ways in which grace sustains us in our passages.

Emergence of the New

In *Woman and Nature*, Susan Griffin tells of an old woman, fierce in her honesty, who asks questions of her mirror. When she was small she had asked the mirror why she was afraid of the dark, and the mirror told her it was because she was but a wisp of a thing, and might get lost in the dark. As she grew larger, she asked the mirror why she was afraid of her bigness, and the mirror replied that it was because there was no disputing who she was; it was not easy to hide. So she stopped hiding. Then when she felt herself growing older, the woman asked the mirror: "Why am I afraid of birthdays?" "Because," the mirror said, "there is something you have always wanted to do which you have been afraid of doing and you know time is running out." The woman ran from the mirror because she knew then that she was not afraid and she wanted to seize the time.[14]

Resurrections are always surprising events; often we do not see how they are related to the deaths that preceded them. Again and again people say to me: "I never thought it would turn out this way." Sometimes a transition leads us to move on; at others, it invites us to stay firmly in place, to discover values we have lost. Sometimes the outcome is new, but not where we thought we were headed. We hope for the complete cure of a disease, and are given the strength to live more fully with it. We search for a new career and end up rethinking the concept of achievement. In the process we come to understand the empty tomb not as a manifestation of death, but as testimony to the possibilities of life. Like the two disciples on the road to Emmaus, even our expectations are transformed in the darkness. Like Mary Magdalene as she meets Jesus in the garden, we are told: "Do not hold on to me." We learn as she did that the ways of God cannot be controlled. When we cling to preconceived notions of what should be, we risk limiting what God can offer us.

What is striking about the movement of the Spirit at this phase of a transition is that women are asked to tell the story, to let others know about the fresh beginnings they have experienced. Jesus exhorts Mary to spread the message of the resurrection, the new life with God and one another now available to all. Mary heeds his words and announces the Easter gospel. The confusion and sadness she experienced at the empty tomb are gone; she is the first witness to Easter.

For women, telling the story may mean witnessing to the hopeful aspects of change. A recent news report describes seventy Catholic sisters from twenty-four different orders who live in a mobile home park, a senior citizens community on the north side of Tampa, Florida. They moved there because their orders either had sold their motherhouse to meet debts or because the motherhouse could not care for all of the elderly sisters. They have a chapel in a white trailer at this Rocky Creek Village, and reports are that their vitality has transformed the fifty-acre village of eight hundred fifty retirees into a tightly knit community. Though the majority of the residents are not Catholic, the sisters visit the shut-ins, read to the blind, push wheelchairs and carry food trays for the infirm, mend clothes for the needy, and perform countless other volunteer chores. One of the sisters, whose monastery closed the previous summer, remarks that the sisters do not want to retire to a convent. They feel a need to reach out to others while they still have something to give.

Other stories provide a similar sense of possibility. In her study of the continuity of self amid change, *The Ageless Self: Sources of Meaning in Late Life*, Sharon Kaufman finds that it is possible to retain both continuity and meaning as we move through the passages of aging.[15] We redefine ourselves continuously throughout life. Though jobs, friendships, health, and family relations change, we are able to connect and integrate these diverse experiences. The values we have held for a lifetime—service to others, spiritual seeking, art and creativity, the ties of friendship—are reformulated in the midst of the changes that accompany aging. They take on new meaning and help us preserve a sense of self. Certain life experiences are crystallized into unifying themes. One of the women in Kaufman's study, Alice, tells how from the time of her young adulthood she was motivated by an inner longing for understanding. Her whole life has been oriented toward probing and seeking spiritual insight. This drive to find something that would explain the meaning of life was instilled by her mother at an early age, and still remains with her at eighty-one. As she and other women explore continuity amid change they show us that letting go is a kind of finding: new beginnings, coming home.

FOR PRAYER AND REFLECTION

1. Wise Blood: A Menopause Ritual

Gather in a circle. In the center is a large purple candle, lighted and surrounded by flowers. Next to it is a bowl of water. A smaller purple candle is provided for each person present.

A Call To Gather: We come together to mark a change of life. To mourn what is ending, and to celebrate a fresh beginning. A woman's creative energy takes many forms. One of these is the menstrual blood that flows through us as a fountain of life. When we cease to menstruate, this blood of life does not disappear. It is turned to other creative purposes. This wise blood, as it is called in some cultures, symbolizes our power as women of wisdom. We let go of one kind of birthing potential to take up other creative works.

Let us join now with one of our number as she makes this passage from dying to rebirth.

Opening Prayer: You who sigh and sing in the changes of all seasons,
   who dance in the movements of moon, sun, and stars,
   who play in the world and weave webs of wisdom,
   Creator God, transform our losses and lead us to life.

Mourning and Letting Go: The woman who is celebrating the transition of menopause names the painful parts of this passage for her. When she is finished, those present call her by name and bless her:

> May you face life without illusion,
>> but with gratitude.
> Though you have known tragedy,
>> may you nonetheless cherish laughter.
> May you have an ever clearer sense of what
>> is important and what is not.
> May your encounters with evil
>> heighten your appreciation of what is good.
> May you learn to meet death in a way that
>> leads you to celebrate life.

Appreciation of Gifts: Those present light their candles from the large candle in the center and then each in turn names and honors a gift of the woman crossing this threshold.

Reading: (*This reading describes Sophia or Wisdom as the co-creator, present* and *active from the beginning.*)

> The Lord created me at the beginning of God's work,
>> the first of God's acts of long ago.
> Ages ago I was set up,
>> at the first, before the beginning of the earth.
> When there were no depths I was brought forth,
>> when there were no springs abounding with water.
> Before the mountains had been shaped,
>> before the hills, I was brought forth—
> when God had not yet made earth and fields,
>> or the world's first bits of soil.
> When God established the heavens, I was there,
>> when God drew a circle on the face of the deep,
> when God made firm the skies above,
>> and established the fountains of the deep,
> when God assigned to the sea its limit,
>> so that the waters might not transgress the divine command,
> when God marked out the foundations of the earth,
>> then I was beside God, like a skilled artisan;

and I was daily the divine delight,
  rejoicing before God always,
rejoicing in the inhabited world
  and delighting in the human race (Prov 8:22–31).

Group briefly shares reflections on how this reading illumines the life passage being celebrated.

Expression of Commitment: One of those present asks the woman: Tell us how you will use the power of your moon-time blood to renew the great circle of life of which we are a part.

The woman responds by describing some of the inner and outer directions she hopes her creativity will take.

Ceremony of Clothing: A woven shawl or stole is placed on the woman, while the following is read:

> There are places on this planet
> where women past the menopause
> put on tribal robes,
> smoke pipes of wisdom
> —fly.[16]

Naming: Since the names used for older women are often used negatively, those gathered may want to honor the woman's status as an elder by choosing a title to bestow on her (or one she has chosen).

Sending Forth: The woman blesses those gathered, sprinkling all with water as a symbol of new life and creativity: "May the wise blood which we share among us refresh the earth and its peoples, bringing hope and healing to our world."

Closing Song and Refreshments

2. A Group Movement Experience Supporting a Woman Through Change or a Time of Struggle *(designed by D'vorah Kost, a movement artist and social worker in the area of crisis intervention in Seattle, Washington)*

Ideally done with a group of seven or more, but can work with five or six.

Form a circle. One woman goes into the center, stands with eyes closed. She focuses her thoughts on what her change or struggle is. The women surrounding her match their breathing to hers, are present with and for her.

Protected and supported, the woman in the center allows the negative voices of fear to arise (the critic, the naysayer, e.g., "You can't." "It will never work." "You're not smart, talented or deserving enough." "You're too lazy, selfish, incompetent.") She voices them. The others hold and remember them for her.

When she is finished, she arranges the other women in a formation in front of her, symbolizing these voices: in one line, or a few lines, or a clump, holding on to one another strongly or weakly (to match the voices as powerful or weak). They represent the obstacles that the woman will have to get through, triumph over. They say to her the lines they heard from her in the center of the circle. She can verbally cast them away, or pry them apart and send them off.

Once she has cast them all off, they circle around her again in support. She voices what she is hoping for. The women form a passageway (two parallel lines) for her to journey through, while giving her words of hope, prayers, blessings, encouragement, affirmation. As she moves through the passage, the women can keep extending the line by breaking off from the beginning and attaching at the end. When the passage is finished, the woman joins the circle of other women and all close with a song of celebration.

3. A Retirement Ritual

Opening Song

Reading: (Eccles 3:1–8):
There is a season for everything, a time for every occupation under heaven.

> A time for giving birth, a time for dying;
> a time for planting, a time for uprooting what has been
> planted....
> A time for tears, a time for laughter;
> a time for mourning, a time for dancing....
> A time for searching, a time for losing;
> a time for keeping, a time for throwing away.

Honoring of the Gifts of the One Retiring: We are gathered here today to show our appreciation for the gifts our friend has given us and others through her years of work. Let us now share these fruits with her.

(Those present express their gratitude, and may bring a symbol of their appreciation, e.g., a song or a diploma.)

Reflections on the Working Years (The person retiring shares her reflections on all or some of the following):

The experiences I have cherished.
The things I regret.
The persons and things I will miss.
The unfulfilled dreams and desires I hope to turn to in retirement.

Blessing with Oil (The person retiring is anointed.)

May the God of Exodus and Emmaus, the God of our seasons
and turning points, be with you in this time of transition.
May She who is the midwife of change teach you to be gentle
with yourself as you let go of the old and await the birth of the
new.
May She who is the womb of time strengthen you with this oil of
wisdom and gladness.

Offering of Spiritual Gifts (Those present offer the person who is retiring a prayer, a blessing, a wish, a promise of support.)

Closing Song, Refreshments and Celebration

Chapter 3

Tending the Inner Life

What Nature did was remind her that ripeness is all, that autumn
is the richest season, that preparing for snow means building a
shelter, that warmth within withstands whatever winter howls
without.

—Joanne McCarthy, "Ripening"[1]

Women are natural jugglers. We spend decades trying to keep competing
responsibilities in balance. How satisfying then to come to a point when
we can attend more fully to the riches of the inner realm, establishing
greater balance between the inner and outer poles of our lives. We may
have focused earlier on raising a family, creating a profession, or developing an external presence in the world. But as the middle years arrive,
there is greater urgency to know and nurture the deeper regions of the self.
For some the image that captures this is that of coming home, a movement
from the scattering of energy to greater intensity. This turn within prepares us for the last period of life when the outer landscape may recede,
revealing even more sharply the significance of inner resources. Then the
task to be accomplished is frequently invisible to the outer eye. This is
especially true when the last years bring frailty and physical decline.

In *Gift from the Sea*, meditations on treasures garnered as she roamed
the seashore, Anne Morrow Lindbergh speaks of the middle years as a
time of shedding shells—the shell of ambition, the shell of material
accumulations and possessions, the shell of the ego. This shedding feels
like darkness and death, but it can be the liberation by which we become
at last completely ourselves. She writes: "One is afraid. Naturally. Who
is not afraid of pure space—that breath-taking empty space of an open
door? But despite fear, one goes through to the room beyond."[2] Could
mid-life not be, Lindbergh asks, a time when we are free at last for
enhancing mind, heart, and talent; free at last for spiritual growth?

Interiorization initially looks like a withdrawal from engagement

45

with the world, a self-serving and isolating turn from others. This need
not be the case. In fact, a strong inner life enables us to move outward
with fewer conflicts and greater clarity. It solidifies our sense of self
and our values. It is difficult to really love others if we cannot love ourselves, and hard to love a true self that remains deeply hidden.[3] What
feels like emptiness inside us may be a self that we do not know, one
that has never been loved. We are like the woman in the parable who
loses one coin out of ten. The nine she has left are not enough, and she
goes in search of the lost coin. Finding our own personal truth is part of
living the gospel in its fullness.

Discovering an inner life may be a continuation of established practices or a completely new adventure. In either case, it includes exploration of some of the following areas: solitude, meditative reading,
dreamwork, journaling, and group support.

A Space of One's Own

Some years ago on a visit to China, I awoke one morning in Shanghai.
The streets teemed with activity, an endless stream of bicycles, pedestri-
ans, buses, cars, and people busy pushing and pulling a multitude of
things. The smell of burning carbon hung in the air from cookstoves. In
the midst of this, alone on a stretch of sidewalk below our window I saw
an old woman. In the grey-blue of her jacket and trousers she greeted the
morning light with *T'ai Chi Ch'uan* exercises. I was struck by how she
had carved out a place for herself alone in the midst of the community.
And yet from my vantage point it was clear that they were never far from
her, surrounding her in all her movements as she gazed into space, bend-
ing, turning and twisting with slow and gracefully tensed hands and legs.

Two aspects of growing older appear at first glance to be similar, but
they are actually very different: loneliness and solitude. Loneliness is a
painful lack of connection with others. It can come upon us whether or
not we are with people. It is the sense that there are no others with
whom we share the kind of understanding that lifts us out of isolation.
Those who are lonely describe the feeling as akin to that of an atom
adrift in the universe or as the conviction that no one really cares.
Alienation and disconnection. If the years shrink our circle of close
friends, loneliness becomes a hunger for familiar faces, for the instant
recognitions that come from long years of shared history and conversation, for the touch that convinces us that we are special to others, for the

presence of another person to relieve the long hours of sameness in a day. Loneliness is painful; we fear it and try to allay its aching.

Solitude is also a way of being alone, but as a spiritual practice it can be one of the gifts of later life. It is a space or time apart, but one held and sustained by a sense of connection and peace with oneself and others. It feels good. Such time apart creates and renews us. Sometimes it means going to a sacred place or making contact with nature. Even when alone in nature we retain our sense of oneness with all of creation.

> Now to take a walk by the river by myself, or sit and write, or stare into the fire is so wonderful. That seems to come with the fifties.[4]

The shift from a painful to a full loneliness depends on many things, including the quality of our relationships with self, others, and the divine.

Loneliness becomes solitude when we can both discover our own inner depths and retain a sense of unity with others. Throughout life we try to honor these alternating moments of solitude and community, to be fully present to others and yet not alienated from our own thoughts and feelings. In one sense solitude is not so much a matter of being physically alone as it is a way of claiming our uniqueness within the web of influences that surround us. One woman describes this in terms of the spaces within her that are filled with the needs and desires and requests of others. Solitude is for her the interval in which she waits and watches for a return of her own self in those spaces.[5] In this sense, solitude is a kind of boundary or limit which enables us to disconnect enough from our immediate surroundings to discover what we ourselves believe, know, and value. We unify and deepen the self. This can happen in a brief moment or require more extended space and time. Such solitude is an experience of freedom, the wellspring of new and stronger directions. Far from being sterile withdrawal, it is the basis of original contributions to the world.

I think I learned this freeing aspect of solitude accidently while quite young. From the time I was five or six, I worked to harvest the crops that grew abundantly in the fertile soil of the Willamette Valley in Oregon. Starting with strawberries in early June, my brothers and sisters and I charted our summers by the next crop to ripen: cherries, raspberries and loganberries, pole beans, peaches, apples, filberts. At times we worked ten-hour days in the fields when the crop was at risk, and some weeks received a dispensation from Sunday mass in order to pick fruit seven days. Years later I realized that my deep love of solitude developed during those long days under the hot sun. My fingers plucked the fruit quickly and automatically, leaving my spirit free to roam and gather. Moving alone and at my own pace on a row of strawberry plants or bean stalks, I could ponder and create ideas, solutions, stories. I came to value the richness and comfort of inner space.

Solitude creates an atmosphere of silence, and this is a necessary condition not only for self-knowledge, but for prayer. Reducing the crowding of heart and mind enables us to center and discover our own inner depths. This is one of the contexts for meeting God. The revelations of the divine are not summoned at will, but silence prepares us to attend to them. Although aware of God's presence in the fields of grain and the lilies of the field, the faces of the poor and the clamor of the crowds, Jesus withdraws from all of this for longer periods of prayer. He goes out into the desert and retreats to quiet places to understand and embrace his mission.

The prayer of intercession is another way in which loneliness is turned to solitude. Prayer for others keeps us aware of our bonds in God. Surrounding ourselves with pictures of those for whom we are praying makes this sense of presence more vivid and concrete. Such prayer not only fills our time alone; it can be a primary form of ministry.

One thing we fear about solitude is what might rush in to fill the space it opens up. In *I Stand Here Ironing*, Tillie Olson describes both the longing for solitude and the fear of what it uncovers:

> And when is there time to remember, to sift, to weigh, to total? I
> will start and there will be an interruption and I will have to gather
> it all together again. Or I will become engulfed with all I did or did
> not do, with what should have been and what cannot be helped.[6]

After years of attending to the needs of others, it is difficult to know where to begin. Even when there is the time and desire, we may hesitate. How does one learn to enter into solitude? We wonder if we have stored away a rich enough lode of inner resources to mine when we are alone. Our next topics help to answer that question.

The Literature of Meditation

Reading is vital to the life of the spirit. In the midst of all the competing values of contemporary culture, it nourishes our commitment to the gospel, grounds our attachment to prayer, and fills our spiritual wells when they run dry. Reading has been a traditional part of Christian spirituality for centuries, long recognized for its power to give direction to the spiritual life. We are shaped and challenged by what we read. Although our choices for the literature of meditation will cover a wide spectrum, there are now many more options for women looking for spiritual resources. There is a vast literature which highlights invisible women in the tradition and brings new perspectives to the stories of biblical women.

Two spiritual practices extend the gifts of spiritual reading. The first is that of copying down favorite quotations and inspirational thoughts from what we are reading. Some women include these as a part of their journals; others have a separate notebook of passages that touch them. During the years I spent learning the pathways of the spiritual life in a novitiate, we were encouraged to develop this practice of copying treasured passages from spiritual books. I can now see more fully how helpful it was in distilling elements of my own spiritual identity. A favorite of mine at that time were the writings of Dorothy Day, especially *The Long Loneliness*. In my notebook I copied a passage from the Postscript, one that I have returned to numerous times since:

> We were just sitting there talking when lines of people began to form, saying, "We need bread." We could not say, "Go, be thou filled." If there were six loaves and a few fishes, we had to divide them. There was always bread.[7]

This book allowed me to cross over into another's story and return to my own enriched. Each of us has a list of such books that have influenced our spirituality.

In my years of working in a nursing center I learned anew how essential it is to have a collection of inspirational thoughts to draw on during dark days. When we feel too ill to read, when we need comfort and encouragement to make it through the next hour or day, familiar passages from years of reflective reading are a sustaining companion. These nursing home years also showed me what a wonderful gift of friendship it is to spend time on a visit reading to someone, and alerted me to the importance of books on tape for those for whom the dimming or loss of eyesight accompanies aging. Interestingly, these last two approaches fit well with what reading meant in antiquity and the Middle Ages. People read with their lips as well as with their eyes.

They not only saw with their eyes what was on the page, but heard with their ears the sounds the words on the page represented. Reading thus meant "hearing the voices of the pages."

A second helpful practice flowing from spiritual reading is the ancient Christian way of prayer called *lectio divina*, or sacred reading.[8] Popularized by St. Benedict in the early Middle Ages, it is a simple approach consisting of four movements which take us from reading the word of scripture, through meditation on its meaning for us, to spontaneous prayer, and then to a silent presence to God in love. Spiritual reading gradually opens out into contemplation. In the words of the French Benedictine monk, Dom Marmion,

We read	(*lectio*)
under the eye of God	(*meditatio*)
until the heart is touched	(*oratio*)
and leaps to flame.[9]	(*contemplatio*)

Although traditionally used with scripture, *lectio divina* can be applied to other spiritual literature. It is a kind of reading meant to challenge not only the mind, but the heart.

The first phase of this process is *lectio*, a prayerful reading and listening to the word of God. I choose a favorite passage, story, or parable from scripture and begin to read. This is not speed reading, but a slow and receptive engagement with the word. It is good to start with a short passage so that we remain aware at the start that our orientation in this kind of reading is toward simplicity and depth. With this, and other forms of spiritual reading, it also helps to begin by quieting the mind and body, bringing scattered energies into focus first. As I read, I let the words saturate and move through me like slow, gentle rain. I am receptive and attentive, perhaps letting words or phrases repeat themselves within me. Suppose I have chosen for my reading the story of the woman with the flow of blood in Mark 5:25–34. I might just let her words wash over me again and again: "If I can touch even his clothes, I shall be well again." Or I might sit with phrases like, "…and told him the whole truth."

When a word or passage touches me, I am gradually drawn into *meditatio*, reflection on what I have been reading. I ponder the word and become aware of its meaning for me. I think about its personal message, noticing how it speaks to me here and now, how it calls me to some attitude or action. I struggle with any conflicts it creates within me. In the passage from Mark, for example, I might find myself yearning for greater faith, or puzzling over the meaning of healing. This is the stage of more active appropriation of the word. We can carry a word or phrase from this meditation with us as a gift throughout the day, returning to it at various points.

As I am meditating, a response to the word may arise spontaneously within me. What follows is *oratio*, an expression of that response in prayer, journaling, or dialogue. As my heart is touched by the word, I find myself in what is sometimes called the prayer of the heart. What I experience may be longing, gratitude, repentance, or intercession. It may be wonder or regret. Each of us will pray as the Spirit moves us.

The last stage of *lectio divina* is *contemplatio*, a silent resting in God's presence. I allow the word to move from my head and dwell wordlessly in my heart. I experience and accept that I am loved.

The phases of *lectio divina* do not consist of an automatic progression. Separating these steps makes it easier to talk about them, but it does not mean that we proceed through them in lockstep fashion. Rather, we are entering into a process that may be different each time. We go with what we are moved to. Beginning this sacred reading opens us to a gift. We cannot dictate ahead of time what shape it will take.

Writing Our Lives

The response I sometimes receive when I suggest that someone keep a journal indicates the power of this spiritual resource. "I don't want to write things down," a woman says, "that would make them real." When we name our thoughts and experiences they come into some kind of visibility. As we write our lives we validate to ourselves and others that our experiences somehow count. A journal provides a record of our spiritual travels; it shows us the patterns, and alerts us to the turning points. Journals are a tested and enduring means of finding intimacy with self and with God.

I have observed two things about journaling. It is hard to begin, but once begun, the process develops a creative energy of its own. A woman who came to me for therapy discovered both these truths. She thought it might help her to keep a journal, but she resisted the process, finding numerous things to do with her time instead. It seemed to her a waste of energy or, worse, a highly selfish enterprise. Gradually she began making short entries in a notebook. These became longer and she eventually found herself filling whole journals, looking for ones with beautiful covers, needing larger ones. She began including biblical texts; letters to God, herself, and others; photos, drawings, and paintings; meditations and cartoons; and passages from books. In the process she discovered the depth and range of her own inner life: painful realities she wanted to avoid, and dimensions of her beauty and creativity previously hidden from her. Her journal-keeping both mirrored her growth process and moved it in new directions.

Journaling takes myriad forms. It may capture dreams, be a companion to contemplation, anchor fleeting feelings, preserve fragments of poetry, chronicle daily events, store impressions of nature and people, or help us sort a tangle of thoughts. It can help us find our way through many of the challenging events we face. Recovering from surgery for breast cancer at fifty-four, one woman made it a part of her healing. She took time to pray, read poetry, and write in her journal each day. The Bible reading she found most sustaining was from Matthew 6:27–28: "Who of you by worrying can add a single hour to her life?" It recurred on many pages.

I tell women who want to journal: Begin anywhere, with anything, and you will find your way. Here are a few suggestions that may help.

1. *Choose a pattern and instrument for your writing that suits you.* Dating your entries helps your journal become a record of days. Write in black and white or various colors. Do not demand polished prose.

2. *Use all your senses to record the sights, smells, and texture of events.* Remember that the depth of life is found in its ordinary details. Notice all you can of life both within and without. Such attention to details is evident in the entry for Tuesday, March 20, of *Being Seventy: The Measure of a Year*, the journal of Quaker author Elizabeth Vining:

> Chapel Hill was lovely this morning with redbud and daffodils blooming everywhere. I drove along North Street past the little house that Morgan and I built forty-three years ago. It stands among its trees (oaks, elms, cedars) gray-shingled with white trim, with an air of elegance, tiny though it is. All the the other small houses built at the same time look shabby and tacky.[10]

3. *Address your observations and worries to God; make them a prayer.* Try not to label the moments of your life as insignificant. God meets us in our ordinary world, and in the inner places of our hearts. Part of Elizabeth Vining's entry for Wednesday, April 11, is this prayer:

O God our Father, spirit of the universe, I am old in years and in the sight of others, but I do not feel old within myself. I have hopes and purposes, things I wish to do before I die. A surging of life within me cries, "Not yet! Not yet!" more strongly than it did ten years ago, perhaps because the nearer approach of death arouses the defensive strength of the instinct to cling to life.[11]

4. *Select just one event from the day.* Record all the dimensions of it as fully as you can. You may be surprised by all that is happening in a single experience.

5. *If you have difficulty writing, enter a single word.* Florida Scott-Maxwell says in *The Measure of My Days:* "I rap out a sentence in my notebook and feel better."[12] Or collect photos and sayings that were part of your day. Press in a flower petal, or a note from someone you love. A friend of mine treasures the diary her mother gave her before she died. It contains just one single line for each day.

6. *Tell the truth about your life.* Each of us needs at least one place where we can do this if we are ever going to know ourselves. If privacy is a problem, find ways to protect it. In the introduction to a volume of her journal entries and letters called *Locked Rooms and Open Doors*, Anne Morrow Lindbergh writes:

> The habit of writing almost daily in my diary probably saved my sanity. If I could write out moods which could be admitted to no one, they became more manageable, as though neatly stacked on a high shelf.[13]

Journaling is a path to both short- and long-term discoveries, a form of self-revelation. It will show you the motifs and metaphors of your life. Though keeping a journal initially requires effort, few activities are as ultimately satisfying and spiritually fruitful.

Dreamwork

We all dream. However, we frequently fail to honor our dreams as sources of information, insight, and wholeness. Many cultures regard dreams as a higher state of consciousness and as fonts of knowledge more important than those available to the ordinary waking mind. Individuals are encouraged to find guidance for life's passages in their dreams. In the Bible, dreams are a way of listening to the divine. When we fail to make room for our dreams, we lose touch with our interior lives and with richly creative parts of ourselves. We ignore the voices emerging from the depths of our being. This contributes to the emptiness and lack of meaning we experience.

During many years of working with women as they have explored their dreams in spiritual direction and therapy, I have developed the following guidelines for working with dreams. Use them to build your own approach.

1. *Record your dreams.* If you have trouble catching your dreams, tell yourself before going to sleep that you want to remember a dream. Since dreams fade quickly, try to write them out as soon as possible after awakening. Even powerful dreams slip away if not recorded.

Record a dream even if you can remember only the emotional tone, a single image, or a fragment from its action. A woman had only one image from a dream as she awoke. It was of a group of women trying to fold blankets that kept falling down on them. Staying with it led her to a long exploration of the deep meaning of order in her life, and how impossible it was to maintain it any longer. Another woman remembered only two brief scenes from what she sensed was a longer dream. In the incidents she is at bat and a pitch is coming. The first time she swings and misses. The second, she hits a home run in very slow motion. While associating with these images, she remembered that when she was a young girl, softball season was the time she felt most fully herself and able to enjoy her play. These snatches of action felt to her like a validation of her current healing work.

If it works for you, use a tape recorder instead of pen and notebook to preserve your dreams. It saves you the trouble of getting up and turning on a light. The recording of dreams is itself a signal to your dreaming self that you take it seriously; assured of your interest and respect, it will give you more. Additional details from a dream may come to you as you record it. It is helpful to have a dream book for collecting your dreams, but scraps of paper will do—and are often what people have handy for jotting them on.

2. *Date each dream and give it a title.* Dates enable you to contextualize the dream and connect it with themes and events in your conscious world. This may be a key to interpretation. For example, a woman realized her struggle about whether to remain in the church or leave was

first revealed to her in a dream in which she was at mass but uncomfortable, sitting at the edge of a pew and feeling that she didn't fit.

A title can be a helpful way of drawing out the main theme or message that strikes you about the dream. Sometimes deciding the title itself illumines the central message the dream has for you. A woman tells of her dream of a big roomy house with the sun shining in its windows. She is alone, but people who pass by keep peering in the windows. Then she finds three women in her kitchen drinking tea. They are friendly neighbors, but not invited; she is upset and agitated by their presence there. While exploring the dream, the woman chooses the title: "Whose House Is It, Anyway?" This leads to the realization of how much her life is out of her control, and how she yearns for more solitude.

3. *Be especially attentive to the emotions in a dream.* One woman awoke with only the sense of a faceless, nameless danger surrounding her. As she stayed with this feeling, it began to connect with a conversation she had had several days before with a close but troubled friend. She realized that she had left this encounter with a stronger sense of the fragility of life and questions about the risks involved in living it fully.

Dreams offer us a vivid series of images, frequently accompanied by strong emotional energy: peace, resolution, sadness, fear, terror, anger, rage. Even when all we remember are the emotions, attending to these feelings may allow images gradually to emerge. What am I feeling in the dream and as I awaken? What emotions come as I retell the dream or explore its meaning? Where have I known these feelings before? What conflicts appear in the dream and what do they reveal to me about myself?

4. *Think symbolically when exploring your dreams.* Symbols work by association and connection. In this way, they take us to new understandings. The Swiss psychologist Carl Jung believed that through our dream symbols we gain access to new realms that balance our conscious view; dreams do not simply reiterate what we already know.

Dreams are not limited to one meaning; they are about many things. A pregnant white spider crawls out of a dark cave in a woman's dream and at first she is terrified of it. After a dialogue with the spider, her fear subsides. She paints it and reads about all that spiders can mean and symbolize. In her exploration she meets the Grandmother Spider of Native American traditions. She finds she is no longer as afraid of her power and has begun to see her artistic creativity as a divine gift.

Rather than restricting and oversimplifying a dream, learn to live with the richness of its message. Ask yourself: What part of myself feels like this person or thing? What are all the levels on which this image speaks to me? Take the key images and make associations with them. Think in many layers.

5. *Play with your dreams.* Through our dreams we can make contact with our creative wellsprings, recognize and make peace with parts of ourselves we have been denying, or find experiences of healing. Think of your dream as a drama and use your imagination actively to enter the dream as first one of the characters, then another. A widowed woman in her eighties became the sad young child in a dream.

> My God, I am that little girl. I *was* that little girl. I didn't want to identify with her because of all the sad things that happened to her. But maybe I can find a way to be her and also a strong and powerful woman.

This dream, in fact, became for her a message about parts of her that were still longing to be free.

Rewrite your dream in the present tense. Carry the action forward and complete the dream. Draw or paint your dream, or one of the characters in it. Dialogue with an animal or person in the dream. Ask them why they are coming to you now, and what they have to teach you. Many women have dreams in which they meet a woman wisdom figure, sometimes a peasant woman from an ancient country, or a woman they recognize and can identify. Entering the dream to talk with her can be a fruitful way to make your inner wisdom available to you. In other words, if you spend playful, creative time with a dream, it will gradually reveal its significance to you.

Inner and outer guides may come to you in various forms: bear, eagle, wolf, swan, beautiful child, Old Woman or Old Man. They may cut across cultures and religious traditions. A Christian woman dreamed of three Jewish elders, or wise persons, who appeared in her dream as "The Healing Team."

In *Wisdom of the Heart: Working with Women's Dreams*, Jungian analyst Karen Signell speaks of dream work as following a spiral path. We wonder, glimpse, know more, and then wonder anew until the unknown gradually becomes more familiar and accessible. Any dream spreads in many directions and any dream can follow another. In searching for the greater waters and deeper currents of our lives, it is helpful, she says, to let our dancing girl, our inner wanderer who enjoys being curious and surprised, lead the way.[14]

6. *Notice any repetition of dreams or their patterns.* Now in her late seventies, a woman pondering the recent deaths of loved ones experiences the return of dreams she first had as a girl of eleven or twelve. The dreams are filled with emotions and questions: Blackness. A sense of nothingness. Great terror and fear. What does it mean to die? Do I believe?

A woman in her late forties describes a series of dreams she had around the time her son, whose serious mental illness had been a long nightmare, entered a psychiatric hospital. She had tried to find a cure for him, and her sense of failure brought strong feelings of powerlessness.

> The dreams I had had for many years of being unable to control my car became more frequent. Sometimes one of my children (small again) was in the driver's seat while I froze, helpless, in the back. At other times I was driving but the car insisted on going backwards down steep, precarious hills. Once my two cats drove the car while I watched in horror from the back seat. In one dream I was again in the back seat, the car was running smoothly through the quiet desert and the space behind the wheel was empty. The car traveled on a stretch of unmarked sand, moving on and on through lavender and soft brown shades of silence.[15]

After awakening from these dreams with heart pounding, she began to ask herself why she was so terrified of being out of control. In the desert dream she realized that the car was under control, guided by a spirit or power that she could not see. She wanted to know this power better. The dream was an important turning point in her passage.

7. *Consider yourself the final authority on the meaning of your dreams.* You are the one who knows best what your dream is about. Consulting books, friends, or counselors can help you reach further insights, but the interpretation of the dream depends on your deep recognition of its truth. Insight comes as we listen to many dreams and learn to trust our own imagination and intuition. Each person has her own individual dream language in addition to the cultural symbols that we share in common. It is important to learn our personal images; this

can be done by listening carefully to your dreams. A woman who left the convent in her late thirties found that this departure had become a symbol for all the other major transitions in her life. In later years when she was about to change jobs, undertake a major project, or initiate changes in a relationship, she would find her dreams filled with images of leaving the convent—anxiously anticipating telling important persons, wondering where she would live and how she would survive, afraid that no one would really understand. She came to see these dreams as an important part of her personal symbol system around transitions.

After exploring some of your own personal associations with the images, you might turn to some of their more universal or archetypal meanings. Many books and dictionaries on dreams describe these. The most fundamental archetype is the Self, the center of the unconscious and the whole personality. Jung called the Self the God within us. When we give this Self conscious attention, our inner voice gains strength and develops further. A house in a dream often stands for the Self; a hidden room or treasure points to the undeveloped and larger capacities we have failed to recognize. Giving birth is often the psychic equivalent of becoming oneself, of achieving an undivided psyche. At turning points in the journey to greater wholeness, women frequently dream of giving birth, or of caring for a new baby. The Self frequently comes as an inner voice of authority and transcendent compassion, imaged in our dreams as a Bountiful Woman, Mother Nature, Great Grandmother, or a Wise Woman. A rose window is also for women a symbol of this Self, its array of beautiful colors within a circle serving as an image of the wholeness that comes from the differentiation and integration of myriad feelings.[16]

Jung believed that the realization of the shadow is part of the work we must accomplish in order to discover the deeper sources of our spiritual life. The shadow or dark side of the Self embodies those qualities that we do not wish to be and would like to hide. A negative figure in our dreams can symbolize this shadow or rejected part of ourselves which needs to be integrated; or it can be a destructive part from which we need to be protected. In *The Road by the River*, Jungian therapist Djohariah Toor recounts her own meeting of the dark intruder.

Some time ago I had the following dream: My husband and I and our two daughters are in a sea coast home on vacation. Everything seems very pleasant until I see a young woman outside who seems to be crazy. As I watch her through the window she walks up and begins knocking on the front door. She wants to come into my home and to be with my family, but something is definitely wrong with her. She slurs her speech, looks somewhat dazed and slightly weird. First I am frightened by her because she seems so out of control. I think maybe she is on drugs or that she might be capable of harming my children. Part of me feels sorry for her and the other part feels afraid to let her in. I wake up still trying to decide whether to trust her or not.[17]

Toor reflects that this dream came at a time when she had too much control over her life and was pouring herself nonstop into her work. She was also keeping a fairly rigorous watch over what she considered to be unacceptable sides of her personality. Afraid of confrontation and cautious about revealing her true feelings, she kept her temper and her thoughts to herself. She recognizes the young girl, an intruder who by all appearances is "out of it," as the opposite of this conscious vigilance. Her out-of-control state delivers to Toor the message that she needs to relax the demands she is making on herself.

8. *Listen to the spiritual messages of your dreams.* All traditional religious systems see dreams as an avenue to the divine. Consider that God can speak to you in any way. Take your dream to prayer and open yourself to its message the way you would to a passage of scripture. In one dream, a woman looked out on a shoreline and saw that it was high tide. She said: "The tide is in." Praying with this dream, she found herself experiencing a sense of fullness, of wanting to age consciously and with a sense of purpose. She became aware that a transformation was taking place in her, though she did not know all that it meant.

It is also helpful to notice what passages of scripture connect with your dreams. Perhaps those with water, or of women being healed and made whole. Move back and forth between your dream and these stories to see how they illumine one another and your life.

9. *Create a simple ritual to honor your dream.* Taking some small or large action that reflects the message of your dream is a way of integrating its insights with the rest of your life.[18] After dreaming of a Guatemalan woman in a long sequence that spoke to her of the unity of the world, a woman decided to renew her membership and activity in a peace organization she had let drop from her life. After a frightening dream in which her mother was involved in an accident, another

woman chose to call her once a week. The ritual need not be even as major an action as these. It may be a recognition that some energy within us has turned or taken a new direction; we are ready to act on it. It can be simply giving thanks for the insights given in the dream and openness to living from its truth.

Group Support

Inner work is enriched by the presence of others. Small groups link women with one another for growth, support, and community. They help us sustain the motivation needed to read, pray, journal, and attend to our dreams. In relational contexts women discover both validation for their experiences, and fresh insights to guide further exploration. During the past decades women's groups have become an intrinsic part of spirituality. They take a wide variety of forms, but those whose primary purpose extends beyond the social and recreational share some common patterns.

1. *Honesty and confidentiality.* This is a basic characteristic of groups that succeed. If women are to risk sharing deeply, they need to know that what they say will remain in the group. The telling of one's personal story is a key part of most groups, and a major source of their power. It can be risked only in an atmosphere of trust. The parameters of confidentiality need to be established at the first meeting, along with the frequency, duration and location of meetings, and procedures for establishing themes.

2. *A grounding in women's experience.* Members speak from their own truth and, as they do, its universality becomes apparent. Hearing others voice what you have experienced or believed, but felt alone in experiencing and believing, can be one of the most validating and empowering dimensions of a group's dynamics. We come to understand both the unique and common characteristics of our spirituality. Individual sessions sometimes include time and guidance in naming and focusing this personal experience, e.g., silent reflection on questions, periods of prayer and meditation, visualization, or rituals.

3. *A circular format and understanding of leadership.* Groups strive for a sense of equality. Whether members sit in a circle or not, whether or not there are designated leaders for some or all sessions, there is respect for the authority of each member. All participants have an

impact on one another and on the interaction. Each also allows the other members of the group to have an impact on her. A common method of starting a group is to contact women you know, with whom you have some shared experience, and ask them to suggest other names. In other words, the groups most helpful to women are mutually created and mutually enhancing.

4. *Affirmation of others.* Though the amount and kind of diversity groups can tolerate differs, those that endure establish a commitment to withhold judgment and to move past barriers and differences that might divide them. This leads as well to greater self-acceptance. Sharing past or present experiences in a nonjudgmental atmosphere helps us learn compassion for ourselves.

As we have seen, the journey inward takes us to the deeper springs of existence. Though solitary, it is not a passage we undertake alone. These inner springs connect us with countless seas and rivers, flowing in and out of them in many ways. Like our ancestress Miriam, who first appears at the banks of the river and is last mentioned at the shore of the sea (Ex 2:7, 15:21), our personal journey is embraced by larger patterns. Discovery of an inner life is at once a way to greater intimacy with self and God, and an acknowledgement of the common well-springs of all life.

FOR PRAYER AND REFLECTION

Meditations with Two Biblical Women

1. A Meditation with Anna

Reading: There was a prophetess also, Anna the daughter of Phanuel, of the tribe of Asher. She was well on in years. Her days of girlhood over, she had been married for seven years before becoming a widow. She was now eighty-four years old and never left the Temple, serving God night and day with fasting and prayer. She came by just at that moment and began to praise God; and she spoke of the child to all who looked forward to the deliverance of Jerusalem (Lk 2:36–38).

You are an intriguing and nearly invisible figure, Anna. Easily over-looked amid the cast of characters welcoming Jesus, so slim is the passage that names you. Yet there is something quietly luminous about your aged presence. You move out of the shadows to offer wisdom for our lives.

You knew how to wait long years, how to let time unfold its mysteries. The rivers of your life flowed back to you in solitude. Because you were ready, attentive, you came by at just the right moment. And your heart opened in praise. Did you know decades of longing, of emptiness, of doubt? What demons did you battle during your days of prayer and fasting? Teach us to wait in times of darkness, ready to encounter the dawn.

You show us how to move gracefully into the season of our ripening, how to ready ourselves for winter. We ask for your courage to wait, your discernment to know the right time, that we may also bring joy to a troubled world.

You learned to gaze into a human face and find the face of God. We reach for that depth of vision. Sometimes seeing is easy. Redemption is there laughing back at us as a beautiful child runs to the back of a bus or swings in a park. Hope touches us as an earnest young man shares his dreams for shaping our world.

But there are other times when a heavy veil conceals the Holy in our midst. Violence and hatred shout out at us as an angry man taunts us on the sidewalk. We scan crowds and find faces so unlike our image of the divine that we struggle to believe. May we learn to look on all faces with the eyes of faith and hope. May the epiphanies of the divine show us how to release the fire in our aging.

2. A Meditation with Sarah

Reading (Gen 12:1–20; 16–18; 21–22; 23:1–2)

As we read of your death at one hundred and twenty-seven, Sarah, our hearts reach back to the beginnings of your story. Like our own lives, yours follows so many turns, is woven of so many threads. There is seldom time to sort things out, seldom words to express it all.

When you first appear in Genesis, it marks a new beginning. Creation has gone awry; it has become a tower of Babel. Fresh energy appears as you and Abraham set off into the unknown, leaving your home to live among strangers in a foreign land. This is the way we remember our own earlier years, marked by a sense of the possible, filled with promise as yet unrealized.

Yet your optimism is tested again and again. You find that you must live in a world where others determine your fate, where famine stalks the land. Oppressed yourself, you also bring tragedy to the life of your Egyptian handmaiden, Hagar. Throughout your youth you wait for God to fulfill the promise that your descendants will be more numerous than the stars of heaven. Then when you have faced the full grief of barrenness and are resigned to it, you are told that you will bear a child. You laugh.

Later there is near tragedy in your life as you almost lose this child of promise, Isaac. Your own death follows the account of Isaac's near-fatal experience at Moriah. Is this accidental? Or did sorrow bury your soul and break your heart?

As we follow your story, we find it filled with both loss and hope, barrenness and promise. You laughed at the impossibility of it all, yet remained steadfast in faith. You were full of years, yet ready to give birth. In the midst of limit and constriction, you faced your incredulity and kept on going. As you ripened with age, you prepared to plant the seeds through which the cycles of life would go on.

We ponder your life to learn what God has done and is continuing to do. You call us to meditate on our own journeys—our times of barrenness, celebration, regret and steadfastness. As life strips us of our illusions, may it also bring us your freedom and capacity to take risks. May El Shaddai, who showed you creative possibilities, enable us to release the power in our own lives, to plant the seeds of promise that will nurture future generations.

Chapter 4

The Ways of Wisdom

So, when we have made every effort to understand, we are ready
to take upon ourselves the mystery of things; then the most trivial
of happenings is touched by wonder, and there may come to us,
by grace, a moment of unclouded vision.

— Helen Luke, *Old Age*[1]

We think of wisdom as a gift of age. What is this elusive and mysterious
quality? Observation tells us that it does not happen automatically; we
can surely grow old without becoming wise. One element of wisdom is
the accumulation of experience and the good judgment that results. But
we hope for more—that as we age we will come closer to the very
meaning of life. We have followed many routes to happiness, feasted at
countless tables in an effort to still our hungers, placed numerous objects
at the center of our lives. Yet something is still missing. "Mid-life for
women," a friend told me, "is a matter of the heart. We find the gifts of
the Spirit within: wisdom, compassion, perception." As women of wisdom, we return at last to the truth of our being, the ultimate mystery of
the universe, the sacred dimension of existence.

In the Bible the figure of Sophia, or Wisdom, is a female personifica-
tion of the gracious presence of God in the world, inviting human
beings to relationship.[2] In Proverbs 1:20–33, Wisdom speaks in the
busiest parts of the ancient city, raising her voice in the public square
where power is exercised, offering her message to all who will listen.
She offers wisdom as God's gift, bringing true knowledge, prudence,
and discernment (2:6,10–11). She promises that when we attend to the
divine message, we will find joy and delight.

> Happy the person who discovers wisdom,
> the one who gains discernment:

> gaining her is more rewarding than silver,
>> more profitable than gold.
> She is beyond the price of pearls,
>> nothing you could covet is her equal.
> In her right hand is length of days;
>> in her left is riches and honor.
> Her ways are delightful ways,
>> her paths all lead to contentment.
> She is a tree of life for those who hold her fast,
>> those who cling to her live happy lives (3:13–18).

In her last appearance in Proverbs, Sophia issues an invitation: "Come, eat of my bread, and drink of the wine I have mixed" (9:5). How can we heed Lady Wisdom's message and make it a part of our lives? Becoming women of wisdom means following her, opening to the divine in daily life. Her ways are insight, life, and peace. We come to this experience of the sacred through: attention, awareness, centering, imagination, action, and, paradoxically, darkness. They are available to us at any age, but become especially important as we move into the second half of life.

Attention

The novelist Harriet Doerr, who in 1984 won the American Book Award for *Stones for Ibarra*, completed her most recent novel when eighty-three. Set on the barren mesa of Amapolis, a small Mexican village of a thousand souls, *Consider This, Señora* examines the lives of four North Americans who have returned to live there. Among them is Ursula Bowles, seventy-nine and widowed. For her, the land is critical. She returns not only because of her love for the place and its people, but to connect the end of her life with its beginning. Now, nearing the end of her days, Ursula discovers at last what life is.

While in Amapolis, Ursula learns that she is dying. She ponders the meaning of this:

> Our lives are brief beyond our comprehension or our desire, she
> told herself. We drop like cottonwood leaves from trees after a
> single frost. The interval between birth and death is scarcely
> more than a breathing space.[3]

Ursula compares an individual life to the stirring of air or the shifting of light. This realization of the brevity of time deepens the quiet attentiveness that already marks her personhood. She spends hours in the village square talking to children. She sits for a time with her daughter by the fire, without speaking, and then stretches out her right hand to lie for a moment on her daughter's folded hands. Ursula reflects that she knows these hands so well that she can recognize their earlier stages in them now. With her hands quiet on her daughter's, she can accurately trace their shape and size at any given date from infancy to the present moment.[4]

Awareness of the shortness of time renders life more precious. This is a natural preparation for contemplation, for living fully in the present moment. The root meaning of the word contemplation is to gaze attentively at something. If we look long and lovingly at someone or something, we have time to capture its uniqueness and depth. We learn the power of the ordinary to reveal the holy. Faith in the incarnation is the belief that the divine is the mystery which pervades and encompasses all things, the grace and foundation of our existence. It is a vision of life in which the entire created order is sacred.

The life of the twentieth-century French mystic and intellectual, Simone Weil, illustrates the power of attention. It opened her to a direct experience of God. While repeating the poem, "Love" by the seventeenth-century metaphysical poet George Herbert, she was filled with the divine in an unexpected way. Weil saw attention as an active waiting for God, as the readiness to be filled; she spoke of absolute attentiveness as prayer. According to Weil, when we are capable of attention, we are led to compassion for all living beings. Love of our neighbor in its fullness means the ability to look at another in a certain way, receiving the being we are looking at in all its truth. We are then able to ask, "What are you going through?"[5]

Attention attunes us to the sacramentality of life and brings us delight. Haiku, the briefest form of poetry, illustrates this. Haiku poems combine the virtue of simplicity with grace and eloquence. Ada Perry, who lived to be almost one hundred and three, turned to raising indoor plants and writing haiku when her eyes weakened and she could not read as well as before. She wrote:

> Pure water lily
> how grew you
> so white
> Rising through
> dark water?

When she reached one hundred, Ada believed she had one more adaptation to make, to the idea of death. But as for now, she said, "I am so thankful for ordinary things."[6]

A friend, James Luguri, who at the age of thirty-eight collapsed and died of a heart attack while jogging, was a wonderful haiku poet. Jim believed that we are already enlightened—and often—but in ways that are so ordinary we find it hard to imagine they could count for anything. In his haiku, life finds freshness again:

> Deep Autumn:
> few leaves left on branches
> freed to fill with stars.

Or, from the season of summer:

> Thin kite strings
> connect a handful of children
> with the sky.[7]

In this haiku we, like the children, experience the tentative quality of our lives. We come face-to-face with a single scene, with reality itself.

Gratitude flows from such moments. A woman diagnosed with breast cancer writes:

> Since the cancer, my goal is to live every day to the fullest. I thank God for giving me this opportunity to be here today, for the people who are passing through my life, for living in this beautiful setting. Whenever the day is nice and birds are singing, I *hear* those sounds, I *see* the Flatirons, I *see* the clouds, the blue sky; maybe not every day, but I try to be thankful for my life and where it has brought me.[8]

Contemplation can be woven into our days in ways we hardly notice. A woman who was recovering from a stroke described how her eyes rested a moment on the tree outside her window, taking in its contours with gratitude. She told how she noticed the evening light as it formed a halo of color around her plants, or watched the bluebirds and hummingbirds near her bird feeders. These moments connected her with mystery; they evoked wonder and praise. Contemplation was not a word she used easily. However, it was something she practiced each day.

In *Plain and Simple: A Woman's Journey to the Amish*, Sue Bender is struck by how the Amish people, with whom she lives for several months, make no distinction between the sacred and the everyday.[9] Everything from doing the dishes and mowing the lawn to baking bread and quilting is a ritual. As she joins in their life, Bender finds to her surprise that keeping her attention steady and confined to a few activities does not limit her; this single-minded focus brings a different kind of freedom. She learns not simply to rush to the accomplishment of a goal, but to enjoy every step in the process of doing something. As with the Amish quilts that speak to such a deep place inside of her, she discovers that this way of living can be at once intense and calm, pared down and daring. The stripping down and simplifying allow one to go deeper, to commit to what remains. Part of the secret of satisfaction, Bender finds, is giving up wishing she was doing something else.

A practice from another wisdom tradition illumines further the state of mind to which Bender is drawn. The heart of Zen practice is a kind of radical attention or mindfulness. It provides another way of learning to embrace the present moment.

Awareness

A core aspect of the Buddhist contemplative path is what is called mindfulness, the art of awareness through breathing and small, ordinary acts. A number of women I see in spiritual direction have been introduced to this approach through the writings of Thich Nhat Hanh, a gentle Vietnamese Buddhist monk. Mindfulness is a practice that has enabled Christians to find fresh ways to fulfill what has always been a goal of Christian spirituality: living in the present and receiving gratefully its gifts. Nhat Hanh believes that each person needs to stay rooted in a tradition, but that we can all learn from one another as we pursue our common goals of peace, love, and compassion.

Mindfulness is both a spiritual practice and a way of being in the world. Simply put, it is learning to breathe slowly and fully while entering with joy into the present moment. It is a way to restore inner peace and in turn to be a part of the interwoven fabric of peace in the world. Part of the appeal of this spiritual path is that it can be practiced anywhere—while washing dishes, caring for someone who is ill, walking in the woods, lying in a hospital bed, driving the car. A key practice in learning mindfulness is to breathe consciously and slowly while repeating a *gatha*, or refrain. When we breathe consciously we learn to recognize breath as a contact point with the air around us and then with all life that has and will be on earth. There are many *gathas*, and their aim is to focus the mind and connect the simple with the profound. One short verse that can be recited from time to time illustrates this:

> Breathing in, I calm my body.
> Breathing out, I smile.
> Dwelling in the present moment
> I know this is a wonderful moment.[10]

Gathas, or mindfulness verses, can be recited during the simple rituals of each day: when waking up, getting dressed, drinking tea, or gardening.

Another teacher of mindfulness, Ayya Khema, says that she teaches three methods of practice. The first is, on the in-breath breathe in peace—receive it from the air about you, from the trees, the sky. On the out-breath, breathe out love and surround yourself with it. On the next out-breath, send it to people around you and even further. After practicing meditation for about twenty-five years, Ayya says that she considers herself a practical mystic, that is, she is both contemplative and political. She believes her mysticism brings her into the mainstream of daily living.[11]

Nhat Hanh comments that in the Zen Buddhist tradition, poetry and meditation always go together. Poetry is made of images and music, and makes the practice of meditation easy. This is seen in one of the mindfulness exercises.

> Breathing in I know I am breathing in.
> Breathing out I know I am breathing out.
> *In/Out.*
>
> Breathing in I see myself as a flower.
> Breathing out I feel fresh.
> *Flower/Fresh.*
>
> Breathing in I see myself as a mountain.
> Breathing out I feel solid.
> *Mountain/Solid.*
>
> Breathing in I see myself as still water.
> Breathing out I reflect things as they are.
> *Water/Reflecting.*

> Breathing in I see myself as space.
> Breathing out I feel free.
> *Space/Free.*

You can lie down, or sit on the grass, or walk slowly as you breathe. If you want, you can just say the last two words of each refrain as you breathe in and out, for example, "in" as you breathe in, and "out" as you breathe out.[12]

Nhat Hanh also suggests a hugging meditation which teaches us how to really hug someone, to remember the preciousness of a loved one as we hold him or her in our arms.[13] If we are not really there when we hug a person—if we are thinking about the past, worrying about the future, or filled with anger or fear—the person will not exist for us. But if we can come back to the moment and breathe consciously, uniting body and mind so that we are fully present, then the person we are hugging will also become real for us.

In his writings Nhat Hanh describes mindfulness as keeping our consciousness alive to present inner and outer reality. Through meditation we become aware of what is going on in our bodies, our feelings, our minds, and the world. We learn awareness of the unparalleled beauty of the moment. He says that he likes to walk alone on country paths where there are rice plants and wild grasses on both sides, knowing that he walks on a wondrous earth as he puts each foot down in mindfulness. Such moments reveal existence as miraculous and mysterious. We look elsewhere for miracles, Nhat Hanh believes, when the real miracle is to walk on earth. Each day we encounter blue sky, white clouds, green leaves, the curious eyes of children—miracles we fail to recognize.[14] When we enter into the present moment, we open ourselves to wonder, beauty, and joy.

Mindfulness is awareness without value judgment. Buddhist traditions maintain that simply by its presence, uncritical awareness is helpful. When we become aware of a weakness, a failing, or an experience of internal confusion we avoid the drain of energy consumed in trying to pretend that they do not exist. Action which flows from such awareness is marked by greater clarity and energy; it comes from a self that is empowered and grounded. This cultivation of awareness can be especially important in women's spirituality.[15] Through simple awareness, we can observe our internal processes—what we know, think, or feel—without interfering with them. There is no measuring of ourselves against some ideal. We can come to know ourselves free of the crippling weight of those ideals against which we inevitably fall short, e.g., we are not productive, patient, or kind enough. The pressure for us to change and become something else is so strong that it is difficult for us simply to be where we are. The practice of noncritical awareness is a means of getting in touch with our experience, of becoming grounded. In the practice of awareness, we allow ourselves simply to be and observe without the need to judge and change.

Centering

Scripture tells us that Wisdom has a double dwelling place. On the one hand, the entire earth is her dwelling; on the other hand, she lives in the human heart (Prov 2:1; 8:22–31). Heart symbolizes the inner person. When we descend into our inner depths and approach the center of who we are, we encounter the wisdom of God. We discover the things no eye has seen nor ear heard that await those who love God (1 Cor 2:9).

In centering prayer we quiet ourselves in a certain way to prepare for the disclosures of the divine image within. We wait in stillness for God's coming. Since human powers have an innate tendency to scatter, it is necessary to center our energies in order to enter into this kind of vertical contemplation, which is sometimes called prayer of the heart. This consciousness of God's presence without images or concepts is often designated in Greek sources as *hesychia*. *Hesychia* means tranquillity or inner stillness, an attitude of listening. It is both fullness and emptiness: the mind has been stripped of images and concepts of God to make room for the sense of God's immediate presence.

There are many methods for stilling the restless mind and body so that an awareness of inner reality deeper than words or concepts can come alive. One path of prayer that opens us to these depths is the imageless, silent prayer described in the fourteenth-century spiritual classic, *The Cloud of Unknowing*. This ancient prayer form has been translated into some simple guidelines by the Cistercian, M. Basil Pennington.[16]

Sit, relax, and be quiet.

1. Be in faith and love to God who dwells in the center of your being.

2. Take up a love word (e.g., Peace, Love, Abba, Jesus) and let it be gently present, supporting your being to God in faith-filled love.

3. Whenever you become aware of anything, simply return gently
   to God with the use of your prayer word.

At the end of the prayer, take several minutes to come out, praying
the Our Father or another favorite prayer.

The goal of this prayer is to make God the center of our lives. We learn
simply to *be* in the presence of God. Gradually this may open out into a
sense of the oneness of all of creation: I am in God and all that exists is
in God.

Though we hope this contemplative attitude will become a way of
life, a way of being in the world, it is important to set aside time to
intensify it. Centering prayer is usually practiced in two twenty-minute
periods, once in the morning, and once in the evening. These times of
silent contemplation do not create our union with God and one another;
they enable us gradually to recognize its existence, to know that at root
we are all contemplatives.

Imagination

Once, when I was talking with a woman who had just been admitted
to the nursing center where I worked, she suddenly began to weep.
When I asked her what had happened, she said: "It is so ugly here.
There is no beauty. I so miss the beauty." She recognized the reciprocity
that exists between our lives and the places in which we dwell, the ways
in which the spirit is fed and nurtured by beauty. It is difficult not to feel
depressed when we are living in depressing surroundings. Care for our
living spaces is a way of attending to the spiritual. Beauty enables us to
retain human balance and wholeness. An American Indian Nightway
Chant speaks of knowing such harmony as we age.

In old age wandering on a trail of beauty lively may I walk.

In old age wandering on a trail of beauty living again may I walk.

It is finished in beauty.

When we are ill or have experienced a number of losses, touches of
beauty, however small, become even more significant reminders of the
goodness of life.

Throughout time, women have been the keepers of the creative
fires, guardians of the hearth. Creativity is a mysterious reality, but we

do have some sense of how it is related to aging. Artists of all kinds show us how closely creation is tied to a respect for the potential found in an actual situation. Whatever the raw materials of the artist—wood, paint, marble—the creative process involves respect for their qualities and restraints. Beauty and freedom arise within the parameters they establish. So it is with creativity in later life. We work imaginatively with the resources we are given.

As we plan for where we will live as we age, we want these places to honor the artist in each of us. One woman commented to me: "The place where I live is so strong a part of me that it is like an intense friendship." We can create places of beauty ourselves; they are not simply the province of professionals. But we also need artists whose vocation it is to understand the spirituality of place, those who, knowing how deeply the spaces in which we live affect our spirits, can bring beauty to our environments.

All artists awaken our spirituality. Through the creation of poems, legends, mosaics, carvings, paintings, songs, and sculptures, artists, in a sense, make the world stand still long enough for us to glimpse its mystery. Like the frame of a painting or the notes of a symphony, they invite us to slow down and contemplate, to notice things more vividly and deeply. Works of art are the fruit of the imagination, and it is the imagination that keeps alive a sacramental vision of life.[17] This is the faith that the particulars of existence can be vessels of grace. Artists assist us in sustaining this way of seeing, for they show us the rich and irreducible elements of existence—the movements and gestures of the human body, the patterns of light and darkness, the interplay of color and texture—in a way that opens us to the divine Depth in all created things. The sculptor and architect, for example, struggle to express basic human experiences such as the feeling of space and the sense of place. Artists provide form for the formless, thus opening us to the transcendent and mysterious.

The imagination is a path to the sacred in other essential ways. We know God through many images. We relate to the sacred in and through symbols which both reveal and conceal the divine. Almost all of the language used by the Bible to refer to God is metaphor: fire, rock, eagle, ocean, midwife, storm, mighty wind, breath of love, father, mother, woman in the labor of childbirth. An image or metaphor is like a lens through which we catch a glimpse of the holy.

The metaphors for God that are most influential in our spirituality both come from experience, and limit or expand it. We find and create these images during the entire period from birth to death.[18] A complex process, this shaping of God images is influenced by religious, cultural, social, family, and biological experiences. It begins in the early exchanges between parents and child, and later draws on other significant relationships, such as those with teachers, friends, and ministers. Once developed, these images deeply affect not only our relationship with God, but our sense of self. In turn, changes in our self-image and our relationships lead to new perspectives on the divine.

Women have never lived as long as we are living today. That means there are no established maps for the divine epiphanies we might encounter. In the middle and later decades we meet God in new ways. There are the agonizing losses and the unexpected graces, the things we thought we knew about God that disappear as life moves on, and the unfamiliar faces of the holy that appear in surprising places. There may be long periods when the God of our childhood disappears, leaving a vacancy that is not filled by any other belief. We become more aware of the depth and range of evil in the world, and try to reconcile our images of God with this consciousness. It is possible for our relationship with the divine to become an adventure filled with fresh revelations.

In walking with women in spiritual direction, however, I have discovered that often another kind of pattern persists. This is the power of early images of the divine—particularly those of God as a demanding judge—to solidify and dominate a woman's spiritual life years later. Like the critical voice of a distant and exacting parent, they hinder her efforts to believe in the love of God for her. Once I was taking a walk with a woman diagnosed with Alzheimer's disease. As we strolled the corridors near her room, she experienced a momentary window or opening into reality during which she said: "I don't know what I did to deserve this, but it must have been something terrible." Before I could reply, she was back in a state of confusion. I longed to free her from this notion of God as mainly punitive and offer her the balance of a comforting metaphor. There was no chance. On another occasion, a woman recovering from a stroke told me: "I think God is punishing me for something and I have to accept it. Why else?"

These stern God images contribute to many women's strong sense that "I am not good enough." The conflict they create becomes especially acute at points such as mid-life and later when a woman cannot demand as much of herself emotionally and physically. The early images sometimes coexist, in an unintegrated way, with later insights about the love and compassion of God: "My God is a hybrid. I have some new ideas, but I am held emotionally by *conditioned* love, lack of trust, a sense of judgment and demand." Part of the pain is that these new insights do not always change this. It is the quality of the connection or lack of connection with the divine that is most powerful, and this is mediated mainly by images rather than by concepts and ideas. The more fully new images of God are integrated into our spiritual life, the more readily old ones begin to fade.[19]

The conviction that we are loved by God can be the gift of any kind of prayer. However, a new sense of relationship is often given to us as we pray with fresh images, rituals, and hymns. Praying with metaphors of God's love and care enables us to experience the divine through these lenses.

> Do not be afraid, for I have redeemed you; I have called you by your name, you are mine. Should you pass through the sea, I will be with you; or through rivers, they will not swallow you up (Is 43:2).

It is also useful to distinguish the divine images we were taught in childhood from those rooted in later experience. We can then more easily choose which God we wish to follow. One woman still feared the God she had heard proclaimed in childhood sermons, but she realized she had come to know another God in more recent years. When asked to name her image for God's dwelling place within her, she replied "spacious." Another woman thought of her experience of God's graciousness in her life and named the divine "The Giver." Moved by what she has learned about the discipleship of women in scripture, one woman has begun to call herself a beloved disciple.

Our efforts to trust our experience in leading us to God's compassion are aided by the fourteenth-century anchoress and theologian, Julian of Norwich. Julian learned through her revelations to move from attention to the fact of sin to a focus on the love of God. As she says, we usually have no trouble believing that God "is almighty and may punish me greatly, and...all wisdom, and can punish me wisely," but we have great difficulty believing that God "is all goodness and loves me tenderly."[20] She saw that the difficulty we have loving ourselves makes us paradoxically more comfortable with a God whom we strive to please and appease than with a God who simply loves us as we are.[21] Julian's experience changed her perspective and her theology entirely. She learned that love is the most essential aspect of God's nature, and that the power of God's love is far greater than the power of sin.

Using the imagination actively in praying with scripture can also be a fruitful path of contemplation. We frequently read the Bible from an outsider's viewpoint, remaining at some distance from its stories and teachings in order to understand and apply them to our lives. But John's gospel tells us that we are to make God's word our home, our dwelling place: "If you abide in my word, you are truly my disciples" (8:31). This brings us a felt knowledge that reaches our senses and emotions more directly than abstract reflection. Hearing the word addressed to us in this way calls for the imagination. Through imaginative participation, we step inside the gospel passage and become one of those in the scene, for example, the woman at the well who experiences Jesus' self-revelation in John 4:1–42. At different times we might become various characters in the story. Entering imaginatively into the word in this way allows us to live in its details until its message unfolds in us.

Finally, play and humor are additional fruits of the imagination vital to our aging. As we grow into adulthood we are taught to justify our existence and prove our worth. We lose the capacity simply to *be* in the world, in ways not linked to productivity. One of these is play. Aging can bring a return to the awe and enjoyment we knew as children. As some of our responsibilities recede, we have time to enter again into those attitudes that liberate creative powers: wonder toward life, the sense of discovery, the capacity for leisure, the freedom to play. The loss of certain roles is an opportunity, an offer of freedom.

Without play, there is no creative life. Julia Cameron says in *The Artist's Way:* "Creativity lies in paradox: serious art is born from serious play." Cameron believes that seeing age as a block to creative work is linked to finished-product thinking. Creativity lies not in focusing on what is done or finished, but in entering into the doing of it.[22] One day as I climbed to the top of a hill to catch the bus, I suddenly caught sight of a glorious sunrise that had been blocked from my sight. As I stood to take it in, the thought crossed my mind: What if all God asks of me today is that I enjoy and appreciate the gifts of creation like this sunrise? What if that were enough? We need to cultivate a capacity for enjoyment.

We also need humor. We read in the story of our foremother Sarah that she laughed in her old age (Gen 18). We are not sure what that laughter was about. Perhaps it was the seeming absurdity of God's message in light of her situation.[23] Humor is a work of imagination and creativity. As in the birthday card that says, "It's taken me fifty years to look this good," humor loosens our perspectives and the tenacity with which we hold to established patterns of thought. Humor even loosens our bodies and emotions and lightens the connections among us. It softens the edges of our cynicism and reveals the nonsense in what appears to be sensible—the inconsistencies and incongruity in all human behavior. Jungian therapist Helen Luke summarizes the task of old age as prayer that quickens the mind and roots our attention in the ground of being, song that is the expression of joy in the harmony of the chaos, the telling of old tales which enables us to pass on wisdom through symbol and the dreams of the race, and *laughter*.

> Surely laughter of a certain kind springs from the heart of those who have truly grown old. It is the laughter of pure delight in beauty—beauty of which the golden butterfly is the perfect symbol—a fleeting, ephemeral thing, passing on the wind, eternally reborn from the earth-bound worm, the fragile yet omnipotent beauty of the present moment.[24]

Humor discerns connections and similarities that are missed when we take a blunt and literal view of things. As in the story of Sarah, humor is an indication that we are still capable of being surprised.

Action

The book of Exodus opens with a focus on women. Exodus 1:8–2:10 tells the story of the events surrounding the birth of Moses. In an effort to check the ever-increasing Hebrew population, the pharaoh issues a command that all male babies be killed. But women from the beginning refuse to cooperate with oppression. The liberation of Israel from Egyptian bondage has its beginnings in the actions of several women who prevent the pharaoh from stemming the growth of the chosen people. The two midwives, Shiphrah and Puah, follow the dictates of God, and do not do as the king commands: "But the midwives were God-fearing: they disobeyed the command of the king of Egypt and let the boys live." The midwives work together with Moses' mother, his sister, and the pharaoh's own daughter, to overcome the pharaoh's evil designs. Moses' mother hides him for three months, and when she can keep him hidden no longer, she puts him in a papyrus basket and lays it among the reeds at the Nile's edge. Pharaoh's daughter finds the baby when she comes to bathe in the river, and she is filled with compassion:

> Then the child's sister said to the Pharaoh's daughter, "Shall I go and find you a nurse among the Hebrew women to suckle the child for you?" "Yes, go," Pharaoh's daughter said to her; and the girl went off to find the baby's own mother.

Together these women save the child Moses from death. God acts to free the chosen people through women who live from conscience and compassion. The story also reveals that spirituality is a community enterprise. It is the experience of an entire people.[25] Even if we are no longer able to engage in direct action for justice, we can support the efforts of others through prayer and encouragement.

As this biblical narrative shows, we meet the divine not only in nature but in the dynamics of human history. Action for justice is a path to the knowledge of God.[26] It is also a touchstone for judging the fruitfulness of our contemplation. Faith deepens through our connection with the poor and the oppressed, and in our work to alleviate the suffering of others. This is made clear in the prophetic tradition and in the teachings of Jesus. The prophet Micah declares:

> This is what Yahweh asks of you, only this:
>> to live justly,
>> to love tenderly,
>> and to walk humbly with your God (6:8).

No exemptions are given for age. When justice is absent the prophets speak of a great emptiness in the country, a famine of the word of God.

Matthew's gospel contains a strong affirmation of the immanence of the divine and of grace as the path to love of others. The criterion for holiness is whether Jesus' disciples have failed to give food to the hungry, drink to the thirsty, shelter to the homeless stranger, clothing to the naked, or to visit the sick and the imprisoned. "Truly I say to you, inasmuch as you did it to the least of these, you did it to me" (25:40).

A woman who understood this path to holiness well was Dorothy Day, the founder of the Catholic Worker Movement. Recognizing Christ in our neighbor meant finding him in the poor, the diseased, the unwashed, the unwanted. The personal limitations she experienced with age became part of her solidarity with the poor. After completing a fast for the victims of famine all over the world, she comments on the special pains she experienced that left her when it was over.

> They were not like the arthritic pains which, aggravated by tension and fatigue, are part of my life now that I am sixty-eight. One accepts them as part of age and also part and parcel of the life of work, which is the lot of the poor. So often I see grandmothers in Puerto Rican families bearing the burden of children, the home, cooking, sewing, and contributing to the work of mother and father, who are trying so hard to make a better life for their children. I am glad to share this fatigue with them.[27]

Dorothy was greatly encouraged by the struggle of Cesar Chavez to create a union of farm workers by means of Gandhian nonviolence. Her last arrest, at the age of seventy-five, was on a United Farm Workers picket line in California in 1973.

Dorothy did not, however, expect change to happen quickly. She believed it was "by little and by little" that we are saved. Her favorite saint was Thérèse of Lisieux, and she devoted an entire book to Thérèse's spirituality of "the little way." This path to holiness consisted in performing in the presence and love of God all the small things that make up our everyday lives. From Thérèse, Dorothy learned that within the mysterious bonds of the body of Christ even the smallest act of love can contribute to the balance of love in the world.

Darkness

God appeared to the Israelites wandering in the desert both in the darkness of the pillar of cloud and in the brightness of the pillar of fire. Our own path to the sacred may also be one of darkness, absence, and not knowing. Darkness is a dimension of all contemplation. For some, this darkness comes and goes; for others, it is the persistent path. In both instances, it can become a fruitful kind of darkness. Women describe the context and quality of such darkness in numerous ways:

> It is as if there were a table in the room with a gift on it, but I can't see it. My faith used to sustain me, but God feels distant now. I believe He is there, but I can't feel anything.

> I fear being led into that darkness again, but I know it has been a rich place for me before. I have a strong sense that God *is*, but I

can say nothing *about* God. My prayer is empty and yet I am drawn to it. My God is now a dark God.

It is as though there is a black hole, a great emptiness, at my center. It feels like a lake drained of water; or as if an ice cream scoop had scooped out all there is, down to the bottom.

Though darkness and emptiness in prayer can be sustaining experiences, it is important to recognize that for many women the sense of God's absence is painful and puzzling. We wonder if there is something the matter with us. We are angry at God or at the darkness. We fear it will never end. We feel guilty, and search to see what we have done to deserve this darkness. This is especially true if the darkness is a loss of a former way of knowing God. For example, a woman remembers how in her earlier years she rejoiced in God's felt presence and had it with her all the time. Then it was gone. She yearned for its return. She was frightened and felt she had lost her way. There seemed to be no one there to help; even the God on whom she had once relied was gone.

The Carmelite Constance FitzGerald, one of the most helpful contemporary interpreters of spiritual darkness, says that she finds a great number of dark night experiences, both personal and social, that cry out for meaning in our time. She suggests we understand them in terms of the category of impasse.[28] In an impasse, our normal ways of functioning come to a standstill; there is no way out and no way around. An impasse is an experience of limits. The attitudes and systems on which we have depended for support no longer suffice. Nothing that we do works any more. In search of a path, we find that there is no path. We feel powerless.

The notion of impasse is helpful because it does not minimize the suffering and frustration that can accompany spiritual darkness and emptiness. Yet it suggests that an impasse can be a condition for growth and transformation—if we face our sorrow and powerlessness; if we can identify and express our anguish; if we can relinquish our demands for clarity and actively surrender our need for control. It is difficult to do this alone. That is why a spiritual guide or friend is especially important at such times.

The writings of John of the Cross provide further insights into how the dark night that feels like a dying is an invitation to new meaning.[29] He envisions the actions of the Spirit in us over a lifetime as a gradual transformation of our love and desires. Our affections and longings are tangled and bound in numerous ways. Through the darkness, through the struggles and the ambiguities, we are brought to greater wholeness. Some moments of this shift might be greater self-knowledge, a deepening of our love, freedom from attachment to an image of self or the opinion of others, a personal confrontation with the limits of all goodness. In the process, our images of God are themselves shattered and renewed by the experience of life.

In this way, what we know as darkness is a path to greater hope and personal wholeness. The dark night is not only a phase of prayer; it is a symbol of the way we move toward God. Like the caterpillar in winter, hidden within a tightly shut shroud which it will burst one spring morning to emerge as a butterfly, so also are we slowly transformed in the darkness. This progressive development occurs through, not apart from, what we cherish and desire. It is our loves that make us vulnerable: "We are affected by darkness, therefore, where we are most deeply involved and committed, and in what we love and care for most."[30]

John describes certain signs that indicate the presence of this purifying dark night. These usually accompany the movement from discursive meditation to contemplation. It is no longer possible to pray with our reason as we have in the past. We experience boredom and dryness. Previous ways of communicating with God through the mind and sense give way to an act of simple contemplation. John's practical advice at such times: trust, rest in God, stay with the experience, do not worry that prayer is not productive, be free and attentive. The contemplative experience of the dark night is marked by pleasure in being alone and waiting with loving attention on God.[31] Anxious concern about our failures and mistakes—the fear that the darkness is of our own making—gives way to faith and trust. These signs can be applied more broadly than the prayer experience, to other experiences of limitation and loss.

As we age, it is important to realize that the many kinds of darkness we know can be opportunities for the deepening of love. Without such support and assurance, we will seek escape, suffer unnecessary pain, or fall into despair. For example, one kind of darkness that I have heard expressed by those in the last years of a long life is a sense of being abandoned by God. The light is dimming and going out, and they cannot find God's presence in the darkness. Older persons have expressed this to me in different ways, but one component is often a readiness to die and the inability to find any purpose for one's life.

I think sometimes we live too long.

I have prayed and prayed and still no answer. I think God has forgotten all about me.

What I really want to know is why the good Lord lets me linger
so. What possible value can there be? All it does is cost money.

This is a frightening and lonely time; it is helpful to know that God is
sometimes a hidden God, that this experience can be a final impasse
leading to the final hope.

It is possible, on one level, to distinguish spiritual darkness from the
darkness of depression and grief.[32] Spiritual darkness is often accompanied by several signs: peace at a level deeper than the surface agitation
and distress, a desire for spiritual experiences and a longing to pursue
them even though usual forms no longer give satisfaction, and good
functioning in the other areas of one's life. In other words, if we are
maintaining work and relationships and wish to stay with this dry
knowledge and awareness of God that does not satisfy the senses, then
the combination of these three signs indicates life and growth. Such
darkness in prayer does not incapacitate us.

Yet because of the interdependence of body, mind, and spirit, such
distinctions are not so easily made in actual life. Some forms of darkness stand out in bold relief as either paths of prayer or periods of
depression. At other times, the kinds of darkness intertwine. Our relationship with God is part of all life experience, and intersects with it.
Depression and grief frequently blanket our prayer and our experience
of God. At such times we know spiritual, as well as emotional and
physical, darkness. Feelings of fear and sadness at times accompany
loss of the felt experience of God's presence. We may mourn this
absence or struggle with depression because of it. The magnitude of
the changes we experience, and their impact on the rest of our lives,
rather than the ability to distinguish one kind of darkness from another,
may be what determines the kind of support we need. In the end, the
same spiritual challenges exist in all kinds of darkness: to know that
God is somehow present even when this is not apparent, to see the
impasse as a call to new hope and vision, to find in the dying the para-
doxical opportunities for life.

These, then, are some of the paths that open us to the gift of wisdom,
whose core is a relationship with the holy in all of its manifestations.

Walking with women who are making their way on one or several of them has taught me that some final words of encouragement are important.

First, all approaches to the sacred are secondary to the experience of God to which they lead us. None is an end in itself. Nor is any the right or better path in and of itself. The major Christian spiritualities are simply the ways different personalities have found to live with and in God. Prayer takes countless forms, and it changes many times over the course of a life. It is pointless to compare our prayer with that of others. Pray as you are drawn. Be free to be fully yourself before God. If a path interferes with your relationship with God and others, leave it behind.

Second, contemplation is not meant for only the elite or the privileged few. It is our way of life as human beings. Almost every person I meet feels a sense of inadequacy in approaching the holy; this is in keeping with our sense of the transcendent mystery. But it is no reason to miss the gifts of the Spirit that await us, the peace, wonder, joy, and gratitude for which we yearn.

Last, we cannot really evaluate our prayer except by its long-term effects in our lives. The point of contemplation is not to experience ecstasy, though that may come to a few; rather, it is to know our connectedness with God and all creation. It is an ancient and universal axiom of spirituality that the quality of our prayer is not judged by how we feel when we are praying. Rather, we know we are in relationship with the divine by the fruits that appear in our lives. Once we learn to see differently, love follows. It is in our homes and our professions, our central relationships and our global presence, that the results of our prayer are apparent. Many people have no felt experience of God. Yet their faithfulness to contemplation is evident in the pattern of their daily living and loving. We know we are drawing on the wellsprings of Wisdom when we find ourselves gradually, over time, becoming more fully the women of wisdom we were created to be.

FOR PRAYER AND REFLECTION

Blessings for Various Occasions (*You may wish to sprinkle the person with water, anoint her with oil, or lay hands on her as part of these blessings*)

1. A Grandmother's Blessing of a Grandchild

May the Spirit of God be the wind that blows free in you, the
water that refreshes you, the fire that warms you.

May you know long life and love abundant enough to turn you
toward truth and beauty, and sustain you in joy and sorrow.

May you walk in the ways of reverence, a friend not only to
yourself, but to the whole earth and all its peoples.

May the God in whose hands our lives are held protect you from
harm and fill your days with gladness. Amen.

2. For Someone in Chronic Pain

God of the desert, suffering God, bless this friend who hurts and
longs for the day when she will be free of distress in mind and
body.

God of healing and wholeness, fill her empty places with hope
and embrace her with your comfort and courage.

Like the woman ill for twelve years who touched the hem of
Jesus' garment, may she touch the garment of your compassion
and feel spiritual power flow through her body and spirit.

We place our trust in you, God of tender love. Amen.

3. In Celebration of Long Life

Blessed are you, Source of all that is, for the gift of this friend's
long life. May it teach us to number our days that we may
have wisdom of heart.

Blessed are you, Beauty that rejoices our hearts, for the wonders
she has touched, seen, and heard. May we all protect the earth
that it may sustain us and those who come after us.

Blessed are you, Ground on which she has stood, for sustaining
her in each season, in times of laughter and discovery, of pain
and sorrow, of joy and comfort. May the blessings of life flow
through us all. Amen.

4. For Someone About to Undergo Treatment (e.g., surgery, chemotherapy)

May the God who gathers us beneath sheltering wings embrace
and steady your fears, comfort and uphold you in moments of
darkness and doubt.

May the God who is our wellspring of life fill each cell of your being with courage and hope.

May the God who is friend and lover keep you secure in the knowledge that you are supported by the bonds of our love and friendship.

May the God who is our wholeness give you healing and joy. Amen.

5. In Celebration of a Long Friendship *(recited antiphonally)*

Let us bless the God of Mary and Elizabeth, Ruth and Naomi, the God who rejoices in our bonds of friendship.

Holy is God, the river of life who brought us together, who refreshes us and gives us joy in one another.

Blessed is the God who holds us fast when pain and conflict stretch to the breaking point the cords that join us.

May this God keep us caring for one another in the sweetness and bitterness of life, steadfast in fullness and emptiness, faithful in our living and dying. Amen.

Chapter 5

Body as Sacred

> I will age like this tree
> Every change a color,
> each move into the interior flagged.
> I will bring light to all parts,
>   ignite thought,
>   quicken spirit until it shines.
> And at last when all is incandescent—
>   I'll go in glory.
> —Marilyn Zuckerman, "Autumn Gospel"[1]

A central paradox accompanies aging. Interior awareness often becomes richer while physical abilities slowly lessen. One autumn my mother called to tell me that the trees lining the sidewalk next to our family home were especially colorful. She was enjoying their beauty so much she wanted to send me a picture of them. In the midst of raising eight kids she had had little time to notice nature, so it was new to hear her remark on its rhythms. The photos arrived a short time later. The trees appeared in all their glory, but with their contours blurred. The tremors in my mother's hands had made it impossible for her to hold the camera steady as she recorded their splendor.

We puzzle over the relationship between body and spirit. How can we continue to affirm the sacredness of the body even as we experience its decay? What will remain of our bodily selves and how will the earth survive? What of the organic changes that rob us of our mental powers while we are still physically strong? Bodily decline is frequently one of the most difficult aspects of growing older. There comes a time when what we most fear is not aging, but disability; not death itself, but the dying process.

Women struggle throughout life with negative body images, seeking to find a way through centuries of idealizing and loathing the female body. Many women have been sexually abused, battered, or raped. It is not surprising, then, that we find it hard to talk about our aging bodies, difficult to like our own bodies and those of friends as we begin to show the accumulation of years.

Women in the middle years describe one aspect of this bodily change as the awareness that they no longer have an unlimited supply of physical energy. One woman said it was as though she had a coin purse and kept reaching inside to take out another coin. One day she discovered that the purse was empty: "I used to be able to go down all the roads, try all the options I could imagine. I no longer have that kind of energy to squander." Another describes the physical limitations.

> It's very hard for me to accept the slowing down and deterioration of my body. I'm a *body* person. I don't like aging. I watch my father, who is ninety. We are the same physical types. He still plays golf, but I see him struggle with the fact that he can't move the way he used to. I'm beginning to experience that.[2]

At menopause, there are further physical shifts and possibly confusing symptoms: hot flashes and memory loss, dry skin and heavy bleeding, difficulty sleeping and perplexing sadness. Our bodies feel strange. It is as though some powerful force is destabilizing and restructuring them.

When these and other signs of bodily change occur, we can deny them and pretend that nothing is different. Or we can hear in them a call to attend to the wisdom held in our bodies. A positive sense of embodiedness as we age enables us to celebrate our sensuality and connection with the earth. It also prepares us for the natural processes of finitude and death. For the experience of bodily decline invites us not to transcendence of the body and the rest of nature, but rather to an awareness that we belong to the earth. Rooted in the truth of our oneness with all creation, we can then glimpse something of the transformation promised in bodily resurrection, in Christ as the firstborn of the new creation.

Friendship with the Earth

We age more easily as friends of the earth. A spirituality that celebrates the great web of connectedness among all created beings shows us how to honor both the earth and our own bodiliness. The whole cosmos is a community of life. Native Americans say, "all my relations," acknowledging this connection to all that is alive. They invite us to look

at the fire and see what it has to teach us, to listen to our breath and
know it is also the mountain's breath, to feel the mountains in our
cheeks just by this breathing.[3]

Connecting our own cycles as women to those of the earth is fundamental to our sense of the sacred. In the words of one woman:

> When we know through our direct experience that we are of the
> earth, made of the same stuff, we can no longer play the old
> sacred game that separates us from nature and our own bodies.[4]

This spirituality rests on the conviction that earth forms a living system,
of which humans are an intrinsic part. The term that planetary biolo-
gists use to describe their thesis that the entire planet is one unified
organism is *gaia*, the Greek word for earth. *Gaia* is also the word for
the Greek Earth Goddess. It is a term used by many who seek an ecological spirituality.[5]

Science and theology are moving closer together, providing a unified
picture of the universe. One of science's most important revelations is
the continuum between matter and energy, the unified matter/energy
field. At the subatomic level, the classical distinction between matter
and energy disappears. Matter is energy moving in defined patterns of
relationship. Even our bodies are continually dying and being reborn.
This overturns traditional dualisms such as body/mind, flesh/spirit,
nature/human, and nonliving/living. The sharp demarcations on which
they are based do not match the reality. That part of us we call mind or
spirit is continuous with our bodies. We ought, therefore, to love and
honor all bodies.[6]

Some scientists speak of life as a cosmic dance.[7] This is a vivid
metaphor for what physicists call the quantum theory. Quantum physics
has taught us that nothing exists in itself, but only in relation to something else which is in turn related to something else, and so on to the
furthest reaches of the universe. The universe is in perpetual motion, as
it were, a cosmic dance of elementary particles. In this view, earth
forms a living system, a living whole, of which humans are a part. We
cannot wall ourselves off from rocks and soil, air and water. All parts of
nature intermingle and interpenetrate. The rivers, the winds and the soil
are inside us. The word for this pulsing, changing, interconnected world
is "organism." Injury to the earth is a blow to ourselves.

An ecological spirituality is based on recognition of this profound
kinship. God's covenant is with all living things.

God said, "Here is the sign of the covenant I make between myself and you and every living creature with you for all generations: I set my bow in the clouds and it shall be a sign of the covenant between me and the earth. When I gather the clouds over the earth and the bow appears in the clouds, I will recall the covenant between myself and you and every living creature of every kind (Gen 9:12–15).

Human beings are called to be companions of all creatures.

Such a spirituality also restores a sense of the natural world as sacramental, of the divine within nature. This awareness is coming, in part, from the pressure of the current ecological crisis, the threat of destruction facing the earth. In light of this possibility, we are called to recognize anew the ways in which nature reveals the presence and absence of the Spirit. The twelfth-century theologian and mystic, Hildegard of Bingen, speaks of the mysterious divine power within all things:

I flame above the beauty of the fields; I shine in the waters; in the sun, the moon and the stars, I burn. And by means of the airy wind, I stir everything into quickness with a certain invisible life which sustains all.[8]

According to Hildegard, we experience the Spirit as the life of all creatures, the connectedness of all things, the fire that kindles all living sparks, the winds of renewal in creation. The divine creative power brings the whole universe into being.

The New Testament speaks of Christ as the Wisdom of God (1 Cor 1:24). In the biblical tradition Wisdom, or Sophia, is related to the whole cosmos. Jesus-Sophia thus leads us to care for the whole earth or universe. As the embodiment of Sophia who fashions all that exists, Jesus' redeeming care extends to all creatures and the earth itself. The power of Christ's Spirit is found wherever we love the earth and its fruitfulness and guard against its destruction.[9]

Bodily Knowing

Christian dualism—the division of the human person into body and mind, flesh and spirit—still shadows our efforts to embrace our bodiliness. The mind has long been regarded as the most reliable source of knowledge and truth, the higher power that charts our course to reality.

However, the incarnation affirms the value of bodiliness. Jesus connects God to the world for all time. Far from separating us from the divine, human bodies engage us in the human adventure in the way God chose to become physically connected to all that is human. In the incarnation the bodily becomes the sacramental bearer of the divine, and the divine permeates the bodily.

We are increasingly aware of how much our bodies hold. In and through them we know much that is essential to human life.

> My own body is going through a process that only my body knows about. I never grew old before; never died before. I don't really know how it's done. I wouldn't know where to begin, and God knows, I certainly wouldn't know when to begin—for no time would be right. And then I realize, lesbian or straight, I belong to all the women who carried my cells for generations and my body remembers how for each generation this matter of ending is done.[10]

Bodies have a tenacious memory of what has happened to us in the course of a day or a lifetime, how we have received and stored it. They contain our fear and dread, joy and excitement. We need to attend to this knowledge.

The interdependence of body and mind becomes more apparent in times of illness. Jan, a woman living with multiple sclerosis at age forty-two, talks about how she moved through her initial anger to an awareness that life is too precious to be eaten up by bitterness, fear, and pity.[11] She describes the worst stage as the moment her legs and vision became so weak that she could no longer continue her work as a nurse in an organ transplant unit. She was immobilized by fear and depression for months. Then she determined to face it: "Instead of running from it like it was a big monster, I decided to embrace it. As long as I cut it off and kept fighting it, I was negating part of my being and not loving myself totally." Though she still allows herself to feel fear and anger, she is getting on with her life. Acceptance has allowed her to do more for herself, to become aware of her surroundings and other people. Her symptoms have subsided. "The body-mind connection is profound," she says. "I've seen people live and die because of it." Most important, she believes, is that dealing with her illness has brought an inner peace and happiness she never dreamed she could have.

Embodiment is a profoundly social reality. We experience our bodies in terms of learned roles and expectations. If society tells us that older women do not climb mountains, dance, or carry their bodies with power, and we internalize these values, then that is how we will begin to experience our own bodies. Health often lies in going against these norms. My friend Ruth, who is in her late eighties, recently called to tell me that she had just been on stage in a dance program. All the other participants were much younger, she said, but "I'm always ready to do new things. I'm always open to something new." She also reported spending time with her grandchildren, learning to play basketball.

When we listen to our bodies we can become good caretakers of our own health. This becomes a spiritual as well as practical concern. In addition we learn to support research on women's health generally, to see the importance of knowing far more than is now available about diseases that affect women such as breast cancer and osteoporosis. These may be the body's way of warning us about a toxic environment. Rather than being merely private pain, they attune us to the web of connections we have with one another and to the need for social change. We honor women's vibrant relationship with the earth itself.

The Body in Prayer

Jungian analyst Marion Woodward describes how central the body is in her prayer:

> I stand with my arms outstretched or dance or lie flat on the floor
> and listen with my whole body. This is my connection to Sophia,
> to the Shekhinah.[12]

Other forms of prayer honor our embodiment: movement and dance, hymns and sounds, lighting candles, anointing with oil, the laying on of hands, fingering beads, going on pilgrimage. A pilgrimage to a sacred place is, for example, a powerful bodily transition in space and time.

Gardening is another bodily prayer. Gardens are not simply hobbies. They can be a way to live in relation with the mystery of earth's cycles, with sacred spaces. Many societies share the universal myth of paradise as a garden; through gardening we can restore a vision of a new world garden and prepare for the cycles of growth to come. Alice Walker writes in *In Search of Our Mothers' Gardens*:

> I notice that it is only when my mother is working in her flowers
> that she is radiant, almost to the point of being invisible—except as

Creator: hand and eye. She is involved in work her soul must have.
Ordering the universe in the image of her personal conception of
Beauty.[13]

Gardening is a contemplative path through which we enter into the
rhythms of death and rebirth, witness the miracle of seeds bursting into
riots of color and shape, know the seasons of sowing and harvesting.
Out of this experience arise moments of wonder, gratitude, sorrow. We
become linked to the earth and rooted in its mysteries. Gardening is a
healing and renewing art.

Prayers that speak the language of the body are especially powerful
when words alone no longer suffice. Some hospices give "hand crosses"
to patients who wish them. These are plain wooden crosses that fit in the
palm of the hand and can be gripped when someone is afraid or in pain.
At such times, sensory identification with the sufferings of Jesus enables
us to experience emotionally—not simply affirm intellectually—that
another has known our fear of death, our treading of the winepress of
suffering. In this mode of prayer we feel connected to another who
understands; we are no longer alone.

In the presence of bodily diminishment it is also helpful to pray in
ways that focus not on what the body takes from us, but on what it continues to bring us. We turn from controlling the flesh to blessing our
bodies for all that we have learned and can do because of them. A
woman developed such a prayer for herself:

> I cover myself with gratitude, using a fragrant lotion.
> I start my praise by lighting my rose candle to Our Lady of
>   Guadalupe.
> My body-prayer begins with my feet and moves upward.
> Smoothing the lotion on I silently say thank-you to each part of
>   my body for what it brings me and does, e.g., "Thank-you feet
>   for carrying me so faithfully, for supporting me wherever I go."

Women also create home altars. These mark the places where they pray,
and enable them to display the sacred symbols most important to them.
The artist Meinrad Craighead has a small altar in her garden decorated
with Indian signs, on which she lights a fire at dawn each morning.
Other women's altars hold beeswax candles; flowers and grasses; icons
and statues; postcards, photographs, and prints; pictures of places from
around the globe. These images direct our prayer. A strong expression of

this sense of sacred space is the Hispanic devotion of the home altar. This altar is usually simple, set up with statues, candles and flowers. It is a physical manifestation of the divine presence in the home, providing a focus for prayer.[14]

The gospels show Jesus as wonderfully aware of the power of touch. He lays hands on people and anoints them. His actions have an impact on the body itself, as well as on ideas about the body. The sacraments continue this action of Jesus, and are meant to be the Christian community's central experience of the sacredness of embodiment, its primary form of incarnate prayer. They are paradigms of the mingling of body and spirit found in all of our spirituality. A friend writes of an especially powerful experience of this one Easter in Japan:

> This has opened a deeper appreciation of the sacraments for me—and our early Easter morning (pre-dawn) pilgrimage down the mountain to the river for the blessing of the Easter fire (a huge bonfire) and the blessing of the water (in the river), and the procession of *Lumen Christi* back up the mountain, is something I will never forget.

The eucharist is a memorial and a celebration of God's bodily presence, and it repeats this affirmation of our daily experience in all its ties to the earth.

I experienced the power of the sacramental rituals in a special way during the years I worked with older persons who had Alzheimer's disease. Periodically we would celebrate the sacrament of anointing with them and family members who wished to come. A priest did the anointing, but since he did not know the residents, I moved from person to person with him, telling him their names. I was struck by the change that occurred as he spoke each name, anointed them, and blessed them. Some wept. Others smiled as their name was spoken, their faces alive with emotion. Some grasped my hand and held it. Though the meaning of the words might no longer be fully understood, the familiarity and power of the ritual remained.

Reclaiming Sexuality and Intimacy

Though research shows that we remain sexually alive and active throughout life and that passion, sensuality, and intimacy know no age limit, the sexuality of older women is shrouded in silence. Further, many women grew up thinking of sex as somehow sinful. This leaves individual women isolated in their efforts to deal with such areas as the search for friendship and intimacy, struggles with loneliness, sexual longings and fantasies, efforts to heal negative experiences of sexuality, the exploration of bodily pleasure, and concerns about tensions in long-term relationships. Couples live longer than ever before. Yet there are few role models or books on how to maintain a satisfying long-term relationship. Whether single, divorced, widowed, lesbian, or married, women continue to care deeply about the expression and integration of their sexuality.

> How long has it been since someone touched me? Twenty years? Twenty years I've been a widow, respected, smiled at, but never touched. Never held so close that loneliness was blotted out...Oh God, I'm so lonely.[15]

If anything, the need for touch increases as we age, and the deepening of our sensuality is one of the paths to wisdom. A licensed massage therapist on our nursing center staff, for example, had a powerful impact on our residents' ability to experience their bodies in a positive way.

Theology and church contribute to the image of older women as asexual. Religious and cultural taboos render female sexuality problematic throughout life, but even more so when women pass the age of bearing children. Yet procreation is only one dimension of our sexuality, and we now live many decades beyond our procreative years. Sociologist Barbara Payne identifies five major trends regarding sex and aging that are challenging the way churches and synagogues see this issue.[16] Because of population shifts, congregations are changing from youth to adult; from male to female; from married to single; from what she terms either/or to multiple choice, that is, to a wider spectrum of choices for finding intimacy; and from exclusion to inclusion, or from the ignoring of the sexuality of older persons, to the integration of their concerns in all programs, rituals, and theological statements. Congregations, she says, have not only been youth and male oriented, but couple and family oriented. The joy of intimacy and experience of one's sexuality must be extended to older as well as younger members. She also suggests support and enrichment groups as well as counseling programs that recognize the great diversity among older persons in this area, and the variety of options open for full sexual pleasure.

Friendships are one of the most sustaining dimensions of love for many women.

> I've a whole circle of supportive, nurturing, loving women friends. I talk over life circumstances, problems and interests with them very openly, receive a great deal of support from them, and give the same. We often have just fun together. I love them and they love me. These friendships have been the most stable thing in my life.[17]

In these years the relational dimension of sexuality comes to fullness. It is time to explore a seasoned view of intimacy.

When we understand ourselves not as an uneasy amalgam of body and spirit, but as a unity, it is clear what is at stake when our sexuality is denied. All our relations—to God, others, the cosmos—are mediated through our bodies. All our senses, including touch, open us to the world.[18] Pleasure brings delight and joy, a sense of well-being. Since our sexuality is an aspect of a whole spectrum of body/life energy, we cannot suppress our capacity for sexual feeling without affecting our ability to feel in all areas. This does not mean that we must always remain sexually active, but that we honor and make room for these feelings.

Our sexuality is a source of our creativity and spontaneity. Its denial, therefore, means not simply the loss of a segment of our reality, but the loss of our connections with life. We instinctively have some sense of this when we note how human touch restores us to ourselves and others; how smells and sounds bring us to life; how time in the wind, sun, or rain revives untapped layers in us. We are only beginning to learn the shape of love and sexuality in the middle and later decades. Its riches and challenges, diversity and complexity, will become clear only as women talk more freely about this aspect of their lives.

Bodily Resurrection

As we come close to our own and others' deaths, questions about an afterlife become personal and immediate. They are no longer matters for theoretical speculation. Questions of material continuity are now questions about us, our family, our friends. As I listen to women, I find that most of their questions about an afterlife concern the continuation of community and relationships: Where is this person they have known and loved: Where is she? Where is he? Will they see them again? What will happen to the earth as we have experienced it?

Resurrection is a social reality. Traditional writers regularly describe life after death as a banquet, a rich experience of union. It is also a work of the Spirit transforming what is dead into new life.

> When you send forth your Spirit, they are created; you keep on renewing the face of the earth (Ps 104:3).

In his letter to the Romans, Paul says that all creation is groaning in the Spirit, waiting for its redemption which is tied to human freedom (8:22). The letter to the Colossians describes a cosmic Christology in which there is a new heaven and new earth (1:15). The risen Christ promises a future for all the dead and the cosmos itself. Evil and death do not have the last word.

In writing of our hidden body of glory, Paul asks us to see the lesser miracle of harvest as a metaphor of the wonder of risen life. The divine creative action makes life out of death.

> But Christ has in fact been raised from the dead, the first-fruits of all who have fallen asleep (1 Cor 15:20–21).

Both in Paul's writings and in the gospel narratives, resurrection is described as transformation. The stories of Jesus' appearance tell us that Jesus is the same and yet different: He appears to the disciples on the road to Emmaus and to Peter and his fishing companions, but they do not at first recognize him (Lk 24:16; Jn 21:4); he vanishes suddenly and reappears in the middle of a room whose doors are shut (Lk 24:31; Jn 20:19, 26); Mary mistakes him for a gardener but knows him when he calls her name (Jn 20:14). Jesus is radically changed. The old has truly died. Yet there is continuity in the midst of this difference. The gospel writers have difficulty framing the eschatological encounter with the risen Jesus; only story can convey this new experience of space and time. Through narrative they try to convey an experience of wholeness, bodily integrity, and renewed connection.

We cannot fully know what resurrection is like; we must live into it in faith. Yet the New Testament is filled with analogies for realities we can know only through faith: parables that tell us what God's compassion is like, images of banquet feasts that suggest the qualities of the reign of God, metaphors from planting and harvest to describe transformation. Revelation reaches us through images and symbols; it comes to us primarily on the level of the imagination. Symbols bring us meaning and at the same time preserve its context of mystery. They are transparent to the divine. This is important to remember, for it frees us to imagine what resurrection might be like, knowing that the Bible itself can never fully describe or literally encompass it. In this area as in all others, we live by analogy.

The imagination is especially important when we are dealing with the body/spirit paradox, for it is the imagination that spans the difference between matter and spirit, holding them together in one act of experience and knowledge. It alerts us to the poetry found in the material world. A Chipewyan Arctic guide named Saltatha once asked a French priest what lay beyond the present life:

> You have told me heaven is very beautiful. Now tell me one more thing. Is it more beautiful than the country of the muskoxen in the summer, when sometimes the mist blows over the lakes, and sometimes the water is blue, and the loons cry very often? This is beautiful. If heaven is still more beautiful, I will be glad. I will be content to rest there until I am very old.[19]

Through the imagination we keep alive promise for the future.

What suggests to us the meaning of as profound a transformation of the material world as resurrection? How do women find hope in the midst of the dying process? In richly diverse ways. Some prefer not to imagine it at all, but simply to trust in a God who cares for the birds of the air and the lilies of the field; they believe that all will be well, though they cannot say how this will happen. Others simply await a return to the earth and the cosmos in some way. For some, experiences of love have about them a quality of permanence and suggest the continuity found in risen life.

The meaning of resurrection is also forged in the struggle for justice. In her poem, "They Have Threatened Us with Resurrection," Julia Esquivel asks us to walk into our fear of resurrection and find life on the other side of the struggle.

> Join us in this vigil
> and you will know what it is to dream!
> Then you will know how marvelous it is
> to live threatened with Resurrection![20]

An elementary-school teacher in Guatemala, Esquivel was forced into exile because of her commitment to justice. She writes from the experience of death as martyrdom. Those who have died live on in the commitment of the survivors. Esquivel's image of resurrection is of an entire people arising as a community in which injustice no longer exists: "It is the earthquake soon to come that will shake the world; and put everything in its place." Resurrection is a social event in which love and justice flourish.

Other women speak of the passage through death in terms of a surrendering of identity which leads to a reunion with the Unknown or God. It brings a peace, but not the peace of possession: "By surrender, I do not mean extinction of identity. I mean, enlargement and complete illumination of being."[21] Our being is changed like a log in the fire. Resurrection is also imaged as an experience of freedom and joy. A friend shared that her mother who was in her nineties became ill and began having dreams of falling into a black pit. When she said she was afraid of dying, they had a talk about heaven. Afterwards her mother's dreams changed: She was dancing freely in a wonderful new place.

At the end of her moving novella, *Tell Me a Riddle*, Tillie Olson describes an adult granddaughter's vigil during the agony of her grandmother's last day of dying. Jeannie has quit a nursing job to watch over her, and her grandmother confides her vision of death to her. Jeannie comforts her grandfather with it:

> On the last day, she said she would go back to when she first heard music, a little girl on the road of the village where she was born. She promised me. It is a wedding and they dance, while the flutes so joyous and vibrant tremble in the air. Leave her there, Granddaddy, it is all right. She promised me. Come back, come back and help her poor body to die.[22]

Jeannie's grandmother bequeathes to her an image of death as an ending that embraces its own beginnings. A similar linking of the cycles of life is found in the work of the Canadian novelist, Margaret Laurence. Hagar, the protagonist of *The Stone Angel*, finds in her experience of giving birth an image of reality that supports her as she dies:

> When my second son was born, he found it difficult to breathe at first. He gasped a little, coming into the unfamiliar air. He couldn't

have known before or suspected at all that breathing would be what was done by creatures here. Perhaps the same occurs elsewhere, an element so unknown you'd never suspect it at all.[23]

Hagar sees that death is perhaps like birth. It seems to the infant like an ending; yet it is in reality a beginning.

Nature offers its own creative transformations as parables of resurrection. From the beginning of time, the universe's creativity has drawn energy from collapse and chaos. Nothing is lost. Constellations of reality change and are woven into others. Visiting the area around Mt. St. Helens in southwestern Washington more than a decade after the volcano's eruption provides an experience of incredible devastation and rebirth. Once a snow-capped cone that rose 9,667 feet above sea level, Mt. St. Helens blew 1,300 feet from its top. Evidence of the massive destruction brought by the eruption is everywhere. Dead trees covering distant hillsides resemble randomly tossed matchsticks. Barren landscapes have replaced once verdant meadows. Yet life is rebounding. Purple and yellow flowers, young trees, native birds and animals now provide contrast to the devastation.

Another parable comes from the Pacific Ocean at Lincoln City, Oregon, where I have walked since I was a child. Recently I explored the length of one of the beaches several times during a week, always at fairly high tide. An hour's hike took me to several huge rocks at the north end of the beach. They blocked my path and signaled the end of my walk and time to turn back. Then one day I arrived there at a very low tide. A whole new territory opened to me within the rocks and cliffs. Vibrantly colored families of bronze and mustard starfish clung to them. Graceful black cormorants used them as landing and launching pads. I could not have known this new world was there until the tide receded and gave me access. All these images are glimpses and suggestions. They do not define resurrection for us; rather, they give us something to cling to as we move through the final transition of death.

Awareness that body is sacred leads us into a new experience of aging. It opens fresh perspectives on knowledge and love. It deepens the incarnational ground of our prayer, bringing appreciation for the devotions that have always been a part of women's spirituality. Within this context, the bodily diminishment and dying we experience is no longer an isolated event. It is tied to the rhythms of all of creation, and shares in its promise of future renewal.

FOR PRAYER AND REFLECTION

1. Prayer of Communion with the Earth

Gather with others before some part of nature—a tree, lake, flower, or blade of grass. Or place some gift of creation—a vase of flowers, a rock, dry weeds—on a table and sit or stand around it. Become aware of your own breathing or of sensations in your body, aware of yourself as a part of creation. Let yourself enter into silence.

Then receive this gift of nature and ask to hear its message to you today. Ask it to speak to you, and let the word or sentence come. Silently contemplate this element of creation, taking it in through touch, smell, or sight.

Then let each person gathered offer a prayer that comes to her from the experience. A period of silence follows each prayer before another speaks. Here is part of the prayer of a group of women contemplating a vase of autumn leaves:

> I believe, O God, that you are an Artist who loves riots of color
>   and endless variations on one design.
>   *(Silence)*
> Thank you for the seasons and their rhythms. I welcome these
>   currents in my life.
>   *(Silence)*
> Support me in the sadness I find in all the endings of my life.
>   *(Silence)*
> As I die will I be like you?
>   *(Silence)*
> I rejoice in trees—the beauty they bring to our world—Thank
>   you, Creator, for them.

2. A Celebration of Friendship and Community: A Movement Experience (designed by D'vorah Kost)

Preparation: Cloth strips are laid out on the floor as drawn below. Half the strips are laid in parallel lines, the other half are rolled up and set at one end. The rolled up pieces should be close enough together to create a tight weave.

Entering the Space: Musicians lead into the space with a song. Women follow, singing, and form a circle or concentric circles around the cloth strips. Pairs of women are asked to stand at each end of each long strip and raise it between them. A second group of pairs pick up the rolled strips. One of each of these second pairs is the anchor person and holds the loose end, while the other woman begins the weaving—over and under the strips held by the first set of pairs. The weavers take care to alternate so that one begins with moving over, the other moving under. (Women who do the actual weaving can be prepared in advance, or they can be chosen at the time of the happening.)

The rest of the women join hands and circle dance around the process

of the weaving. Musicians play and songs are sung. One possible chant is: "We are the flow, we are the ebb; we are the weaver, we are the web."

When the web is completed, there is a closing circle dance with the women alternating in holding it aloft, moving it as they move. Those holding the cloth can raise and lower and billow it, can turn around with it, can bring it over all the women as a sheltering presence. It becomes the web of life held aloft by the breath of the Spirit, a shelter of peace, a symbol of the oneness of all creation, or of the joining of all individual gifts in community.

Possible Variations: The cloth strips can be a variety of colors to create a rainbow effect. The length can vary, but fifteen feet works well. If the group is too large for one weaving, make two weavings simultaneously, or three or four, all within one large circle or within separate circles.

If a light color is used, indelible markers can be available for women to write hopes, dreams, or favorite sayings on the cloth. If more verbal involvement is desired, the women who take hold of the streamers can

alternate with statements, e.g., speaking as a woman of history, naming her own matrilineage, saying a prayer, or offering a blessing to all present.

If desired, eight- to nine-inch thin strips cut from the same fabric can be passed out to each woman. At the beginning of the gathering, each turns to another woman and ties her small strip around the wrist of the other, symbolizing each one's connectedness with the greater whole. She may say a wish, a prayer, or blessing for the other woman as she ties on the strip.

Chapter 6

Seasons of Mourning

In black there are all colors.
Where darkness always the light.
Iridescent the raven's wing in sunlight.
—Brooke Medicine Eagle, "Women and Nature"[1]

If depth and beauty grow more intense with age, so does the darkness. We know more of both the bitter and the beautiful; often the two are intertwined. One shape the darkness takes is loss. We endure losses all of our lives, of course. Some are small, and we hardly notice them. Yet there comes a time for most of us when losses become more frequent, overlapping, and irreplaceable. We learn how intrinsic pain and suffering are to love. The experience of loss threatens both who we are and how we care. To preserve both, we must learn how to mourn all kinds of losses.

Though the tapestry of mourning differs for each individual and event, there are common threads. Identifying these can help us both understand the nature of grief and support the grieving process itself. We need such understanding to guide us personally through the experience of loss, and to help us walk with friends and relatives in times of sorrow. In our reflections, we will turn most often to the experience of losing a loved one in death. What is true of that experience applies in different ways to other kinds of mourning.

Understanding Grief

Mourning is a natural healing process. It moves in its own way and at its own pace. In *A Book About My Mother*, Toby Talbot describes her loss:

Mourning has a path of its own. A route which does not move in one straight line. Some days I can look at her photograph and the

104

image revives her, reinforces her for me. On other days I gaze at
her and am blinded with tears.[2]

Amid many variations grief nonetheless follows a general path. It takes
us through a period of numbness or shock, into a time of disconnection
and confusion, and to new ways of connecting with self and others. We
may circle through this process many times; often it is like being buf-
feted by ocean waves.

1. *Feeling Shock and Disbelief.* When we first learn of a large loss, it
is nearly impossible to take it in: saying goodbye to a house and
belongings we have cherished for years; the vanishing of the ability to
walk, see, or remember; the sudden disappearance of a person's quick
laughter, warm touch, and keen mind. We cannot wrap our hearts and
minds around the reality that this object, ability, or person is gone. The
news hangs over body, mind, and spirit like a deep winter chill. The
poet Emily Dickinson captures the feeling of it.

> This is the Hour of Lead—
> Remembered, if outlived,
> As Freezing persons, recollect the Snow—
> First—Chill—then Stupor—then the letting go—[3]

During this time, it is hard to think and function. We are dazed and dis-
believing, and we may wonder if we have imagined or dreamed what is
happening. A woman who had been told that her favorite granddaughter
was struck by a car in a distant city dialed her daughter back almost
immediately. "Did you really just call to tell us that Natalie was rushed
to the hospital?" she asked. "I'm afraid so, mom," her daughter replied.

Yet this numbness protects us. We cannot embrace a major loss all at
once. For lesser losses, the effects of this initial anesthesia may wear off
more quickly. Gradually, with all kinds of losses, we need to let the
reality in. Once I was called to the apartment of a woman living in the
retirement complex where I worked. Her son had been cleaning out the
basement of his house and had brought her a box of things discovered
there. In it she found old cards and love letters from her husband who
had died several years earlier. When she reread them, her sadness surfaced again, and she did not want to be alone with it. As we talked
about him, she told me that at the time of his death she did not at first
allow herself to feel anything. She had gone through the funeral in a

way that friends praised as very courageous. Months later she had cleaned out some of his belongings and put them in bags outside near her garbage can. The next morning she awoke just as the garbage men were lifting the large bags and tossing them into their truck. It was then that her sorrow broke from her, and she began to sob.

2. *Falling Apart.* As the actuality of a loss sinks in, we begin the task of expressing and working through all aspects of it. Like some friends of ours whose house burned down, we learn only as the days go by that we are missing certain things. The self and world we have known disintegrate. We fall apart. Culture and families make grief more difficult when they admire the person who holds it all together, who takes it well. This is just the opposite of what needs to happen if we are to heal. There is no way around the pain; we must go through it. If those close to us cannot handle this, we will hide our feelings instead of expressing them. A client, recounting to me her overwhelming sadness at the funeral of a lifelong friend, said how hard it was for her that few others were showing their sorrow. She was embarrassed by the strength of her emotions. "I wish we had official mourners," she said, "so that it would be OK for us to make noise."

When we begin to mourn a loss, the heart and mind break it into fragments. We turn over each of these many times and, as we do, a confusing and contradictory array of feelings erupt. We may yearn and long for what is gone: "I'd give anything to hear his voice just one more time." There may be periods of unfocused rage at the unfairness of it all, or times of more focused anger directed at doctors, friends, the person who has died. We are haunted by our own shortcomings and the ways in which we failed the person. When we see beauty or goodness we think of how they would have enjoyed it. Sometimes we wake early in the morning with hearts full of heaviness and dread. Sadness wells up at unexpected times and places. There are brief moments of forgetfulness, but then the feelings sweep over us again. Some of the feelings seem unreasonable: Why should we feel angry with people who are trying to do their best? Why do we resent the health and happiness of others, their ability to go about daily tasks as though nothing had happened? How can we be grateful at one moment and so sad the very next? Will we go on weeping forever?

The world no longer feels the same; the fragility of all things and people is apparent. The veil between life and death becomes thin. If we can lose something or someone we love, the universe is a precarious and dangerous place. It is hard to trust. We may have panic and anxiety attacks.

Grieving is a bodily process, since emotions lie deep in our physical being. We may experience great fatigue; headaches and muscle pains; inner chills; difficulty concentrating, sleeping, and eating. There may also be bursts of physical energy which we are driven to burn off by walking or cleaning house until we drop from exhaustion. Since we are vulnerable to illness during grief, it is important to take care of our bodies and see a doctor for symptoms that trouble us.

More than anything else during this period, we need to hear that it will end. The pain will not last forever. We will get through it. Just as the first crocus signals the coming of spring, so one day the stirrings of new energy will tell us that we are ready to move on.

3. *Connecting Again.* Through the process of mourning we come to a new self, one that has now incorporated the loss. Out of the period of disintegration we move to a reintegration of the parts of our lives. We are never the same again after a significant sorrow, but at some point we begin to reconnect. There is interest in reaching out, forming new relationships, investing in life.

> Piece by piece, I reenter the world. A new phase. A new body, a new voice. Birds console me by flying, trees by growing, dogs by the warm patch they leave on the sofa. Unknown people by performing their motions. It's like a slow recovery from a sickness, this recovery of one's self.[4]

This reconnecting happens on many levels. Not only do we recover parts of ourselves, we find energy to relate again to others. We can experience joy and love without guilt. We become active in the communities to which we belong, and find new sources of interest. We search for ways to turn tragedies into something life-giving. Reintegration also means incorporating a beloved object or person into our present life in new and enriching ways. The form of their presence and our connections with them have been transformed.

This, then, is the broad path: shock, disintegration, reintegration. Two metaphors help me image the process. Grief is like a spiral staircase. We circle back again and again to the same floors, trying fully to take in all their furnishings, examining everything from many vantage points. This doubling back allows us to deepen the meaning of the loss.

Experiences alter as we journey through them. Frequently the places we return to are those most difficult for us to integrate. Or, in a different metaphor, grieving is like tending to a wound. Sometimes the wound heals badly and we must reopen and drain it so that it can heal well. While it is healing, the energy of mind and body focus on this weakened place and we feel too exhausted to invest in other things. There is a time of more intense pain and when that is past we return to normal functioning. A scar remains, however.

> Certain smells, certain moments when I feel unloved, certain aspects of the Christmas rituals, and hundreds of other ordinary details of life, will reopen the wound. But at least now I can let it bleed for a while and go on. At least now I can be open, not only to those painful moments, but also to the many joys of my life.[5]

Though eventually healed, the sorrow remains forever a part of us.

Supporting the Grieving Process

Once we understand something of the movement of mourning, questions arise: What will help me make it through the pain? How can I attune myself well to the rhythm of my own healing process? How will it affect my faith in myself, in God? From my own experience of grieving, as well as that of being a companion to other women, I see the following as especially important.

1. *Locating a reverent listener.* In the midst of grief we are filled with emotions that need expression. A central aspect of mourning is finding a way to release them: in tears, screams, and sobs; by talking with others; through writing in a journal; by creating poetry, ritual, or music. Telling the story of the loss over and over again, with freedom to say fully what it means, is how we heal. This goes best when we have a companion, someone who is not afraid of our emotions and can hold our pain. In their presence our inner feelings are no longer unacceptable.

Support groups can also be helpful places to grieve, especially when we find there others going through a similar experience: widows, parents who have lost children, others diagnosed with a chronic or terminal illness such as ours. If our loss is one that has been long buried and never grieved until now, if we are mourning a childhood trauma, or if our process becomes stuck or life-threatening, we should find a counselor or other professional trained to walk with us during such times.

We often discover in sharing a loss, that we are reexperiencing other losses past and present. Sorrow has its own lines of association, and when we grieve one loss we find ourselves grieving all our losses. Upon hearing of the death of her sister in a nursing home, a woman's sadness was not so much for the death—which she considered a blessing—but for this sister's hard life. She had married an alcoholic and abusive husband, and lived with Parkinson's disease for years. "I don't know," the woman said, "that night, when I went to bed, in my heart I just wanted to sob for my sister's life."

When we are the one listening, we may feel inadequate. It is hard to know what to do or say in the face of great sorrow.

> Mary Magdalene struggled and sobbed,
> The best-loved disciple was turned to rock
> But there where the silent Mother stood,
> There, no one dared to look.[6]

We are tempted to turn away from someone in grief. Once able to conquer our desire to flee, we find that silence has its own power. We remember the solace of a listening heart, the significance of even a speechless presence. We do not need to give advice, explanations, or answers. We just need to be there.

2. *Keeping faith with God.* Grief affects everything, including our friendship with God. While we may continue to experience God's presence during a loss, it is not unusual to find that we can no longer pray, that we are angry with God, or that there is a veil between us. We have no felt sense of divine comfort. Established forms of prayer are no longer possible. Questions of Why? Why me? and Why this? arise in our hearts. We struggle before the mystery of suffering and evil, unable to find comfort in any system of explanation: "I have all these questions. I know there are these millions and billions of people and I wonder how God can be watching over my own little bunch. But otherwise there is just darkness. There is this enormous mystery." Our relationship with God is being transformed in the crucible of sorrow.

Religious platitudes do not help us during grief and, in fact, may block or hinder our process. A friend whose husband had died suddenly in his sleep told me she had a book she wanted me to write. "Warn widows," she said, "about all the difficult things well-meaning friends will say to them in the name of religion." Her list included: "God will make it all right for you." "God never sends us more than we can handle." "It must have been God's will that he go now."

What does help is the freedom to be completely ourselves before God, and to pray in whatever way we can. Clinging to the silence. Crying out in anger and pain. Asking God to witness our loss. Shedding the tears we cannot weep elsewhere. Holding to faith in the darkness. Repeating familiar chants or short prayers. Another path to prayer is to allow ourselves to be more active: to walk, to move about, to cease trying to sit still when it has become impossible. At such times we also need set forms of prayer that sustain us with their rhythms when we are unable to formulate any words: the good shepherd psalm (23), the stations of the cross, the rosary.

During her husband's battle with cancer, Madeleine L'Engle says that as she swam every morning before breakfast, she silently recited various verses she had memorized. The movement of her body through the water helped her mind and heart work together. When she had finished her memorized alphabet of poems and prayers, she had swum for over half an hour, sustained by the deep rhythm of faith found in these affirmations.[7] In an interview the year before she died of breast cancer Sister Thea Bowman describes how she drew on traditional black prayer in a similar way:

> My people used to say—and still say—sometimes you have to moan. I remember old people sitting out on their porches and moaning on and on in a kind of deep, melodic hum. I've found that moaning is therapeutic. It's a way of centering, the way you do in centering prayer. You concentrate your internal energies and your powers in prayer or wordless outcry to God. Old people used to say the words from Scripture, "When we don't know how to pray, the Spirit intercedes for us with inexpressible groaning." So, sometimes you just moan.[8]

God is there in the healing itself. Where to go next will be given us.

3. *Believing in love in the midst of human tragedy.* As women speak of the sadness threatening to envelop them, one layer is almost always awareness of global suffering and evil. With the passage of years we become intimately acquainted with tragedy. Unfair and unjustifiable suffering deeply challenges our belief in God. The explanations of philosophers over the ages echo hollowly in our hearts when we are per-

sonally close to such suffering. Our inability to accomplish significant improvements in the world troubles us. We mourn.

This concern for the pain of the world is a recognition of our interconnectedness. Even when at peace about our own lives, we are conscious of the massive distress of people everywhere. In her poem, "One," Sister Bernadette Carlson speaks of such world-sorrow:

> I wait dark's discerning:
> Borders open on streaming peoples,
> bowed pain. My shade their shadow.
> I would find the way I must walk
> or be stranger to all those names
> wearing in mirror image a face I know.[9]

Our hearts are heavy and we feel powerless to affect such large-scale events.

There is tragedy and evil that resist all explanation and justification.[10] This has perhaps been true at all times, but with the technology available to us we can learn in helpless horror of the death of innocent children in Bosnia, and the torment of never knowing felt by the mothers of the "disappeared" in El Salvador. The scope and intensity of this suffering are intolerable and threaten to plunge us into despair. With the prophets we wrestle with God in light of this injustice.

> Our holy and beautiful house,
> Where our ancestors praised you,
> is burned to the ground;
> all that gave us pleasure lies in ruins.
> God, can you go unmoved by all of this,
> oppressing us beyond measure by your silence?
> (Is 64:10–12)

We may try to live as though this suffering did not exist, since we can find no way to understand it. This may work for a while, but it means narrowing the scope of our attention and concern. There is another path, one that expands rather than constricts our vision. The way out of this despair is through a compassion that resists evil and suffering. Some of the conditions for such suffering can be identified and addressed. There is no way to compensate for tragedy, but we can transform the meaning of personal tragedy by making it the basis for social action. Finding in it a gift for others is a way to transcend it. This action may focus on others who have experienced a similar tragedy or be a contribution to a wider order of justice.

> I want women to have some sense of hope, because I can just remember how terrifying it was not to have any hope—the days I felt there was no way out. I feel very much like that's part of my mission, part of why God didn't allow me to die in that marriage, so that I could talk openly and publicly—and it's taken me so many years to be able to do it—about having been battered.[11]

Such actions do not give us the sense that evil has been overcome; rather, they assure us that there is still love in the world. We take whatever steps are possible and continue to work in spite of the smallness of results. Hope is born in such community; when our faith falters, someone else's may be holding firm. My action may be small but it gains momentum when combined with those of others.

When we have done all that we can to resist such suffering, when we find that the disease is incurable, the situation hopeless, practical efforts useless, then we can still do all in our power to prevent the circumstances from destroying or degrading our humanity and that of others. We do this by offering all of the comfort, empowerment and support possible in the given circumstances. This is the meaning of incarnation.

It is incarnation that sustains us, the sacrament of God's love found in the love and support of others. When we look around for God's presence and cannot find it, we are reminded that it is in us. Or as close to us as those people who reach out to us and others, who continue in spite of deep discouragement to work for peace in war-torn lands, who in countless ways keep inserting love into a world that is so in need of healing.

One source of comfort is the knowledge that a compassionate God is with us in the suffering, that God does not send it to us, but struggles with us against it and works with us to bring all possible good out of tragedy.[12] At the points of deepest suffering, God is our ally in resistance, not a judge who sends the suffering as trial or punishment. When we connect with this God in prayer, we can more readily bear the suffering we see. Jesus cried out the words of the psalmist, "My God, my God, why have you forsaken me?" We can feel free to speak that prayer as well. When we go deep enough, we find a point from which we can live with the experience.

Faith is a deep wellspring that we know is there even when it does not lessen the pain of the suffering. It is the water that flows beneath the surface to which we sometimes can return for sustenance. It does not extinguish our awareness of the senseless suffering in the world. But deeper than this darkness of evil there is a vision of the compassion of God. In the story of Job, it is not the arguments of his friends that bring him solace, but the momentary reminders of the magnificence and beauty of the universe and above all, the experience of God's presence and love. It is some such experience that will enable us to feel the pain and grief of the world without being destroyed by it.

> Though the fig tree does not blossom,
> nor fruit be on the vines,
> the produce of the olive fail
> and the fields yield no food,
> the flock be cut off from the fold
> and there be no herd in the stalls,
> yet I will rejoice in God,
> I will joy in the God of my salvation.
> God is my strength and
> makes my feet like hinds' feet,
> makes me tread upon my high places (Hab 3:17–19).

Finally, we leave to God all that we can do nothing about.

4. *Losing and finding a self.* As an older friend prepares to leave her home, she sits and weeps. She needs to relocate to a retirement complex. She is not well, and if she does not move near her children, she will have no one to monitor what happens and speak up for her. But the move will take her to a completely different part of the country, away from the ocean and mountains she loves. How can she be the same without them? How will anyone know who she is in a completely new setting? She decides to take a scrapbook with her, to tell people about herself:

> I think we all should. At 75 I think we should wear a button with
> a picture of ourselves, so people will know who we are, what we
> were, what we bring with us that they cannot see.

My friend has always been a woman of prayer, drawing sustenance from the words of scripture. Now she struggles to understand what Jesus means by saying that if we want to save our lives we must lose them.

In her journals, novelist and poet May Sarton tells us that she also wrestles with this paradox of finding and losing a self. In *At Seventy*, she recounts a talk she gave on old age at Hartford College in Connecticut as part of a series on the seasons of a woman's life. During the course of the talk she says: "This is the best time of my life. I love being old." When someone in the audience asks loudly, "Why is it good to be old?" she replies: "Because I am more myself than I have ever been. There is less conflict. I am happier, more balanced, and...more power-ful."[13] She meant, Sarton says, that she was more able to use her powers, that she had less self-doubt to conquer and more certainty of what life is all about.

At the time of that talk, Sarton was feeling well, working on a new novel and writing poems. Then, when she was seventy-three, she suf-fered a stroke and endured nine months in which she could not write or garden, and was in and out of the hospital. Illness made a marked differ-ence. In *After the Stroke*, Sarton comments that everyone she talks to on the phone says that she sounds wonderfully herself. She cannot find a way to tell them that she is *not* her self; she cannot respond as she once could and her vitalizing solitude has turned to feelings of being aban-doned and desolate: "Loneliness because in spite of all the kindnesses and concern of so many friends there was no one who could fill the hole at the center of my being—only myself could fill it by becoming whole again. It was loneliness in essence for the *self*."[14] Physical frailty makes artistic creation difficult. She is often too sick to do anything and cannot find the poet within herself; she feels disoriented, without an identity.

In *Endgame*, Sarton chronicles her seventy-ninth year, when illness strikes her heart and lung, draining energy from her body and consum-ing her in the battle for health: "If someone found their way here, as has only happened once since I moved in seventeen years ago, and said they were looking for May Sarton my answer would have to be 'She did live here but she is not here now.'"[15] Even viewing the sea or visiting her garden to see the flowers and hear the birds becomes a painful effort. She finds herself crying from frailty, out of shame at having so little strength and being unable to do things that she wants very much to do. But she begins slowly re-creating a person, the person she is now. No longer able to work at her typewriter, Sarton learns to dictate into a machine. She writes with her voice and lets others put the words on paper. It is the record, as she puts it, of learning to become dependent: "This has been the struggle of the last months, to learn to accept that my life as writer is probably over and to learn to accept dependence."[16]

Yet another change occurs as Sarton reaches her eightieth year. Her journal *Encore* begins with her seventy-ninth birthday, which she thinks might be her happiest ever. Physical struggles continue: small things take longer, she tires easily, her body feels fragile and ill, she is depressed and in pain. It is a dark passage. But energy is there on other days and her spirits lift. She returns to her garden, enjoys friendships, writes poetry. Sarton sums up her reflections by saying that she has lived through a thicket of ill-health into a time of extraordinary happiness and fulfillment. It is more than she dreamed possible. She ends her journal with some favorite lines from the poet George Herbert: "And now in age I bud again,/After so many deaths I live and write."[17]

This process of losing and finding a self changes with the nature of our losses. Sometimes it is like my friend's efforts to be fully known in a new setting; at others, like May Sarton's struggle to find fullness in the midst of increasing physical diminishment. When the loss we are mourning is the death of a person close to us, we may also find a new sense of self through a transformation of that relationship. Many have shared with me experiences of the dead person present in a new way and of the reassurance this brings them: a dead husband sits at the edge of their bed as they awaken in the morning; a father recently deceased appears briefly in the kitchen chair—and then is gone; the love of a friend who has died is strong and unmistakable. There is no image, but a new peace remains after the presence fades. The dead person may also come in a dream, whole and healed, no longer suffering, sometimes at a younger age: a friend lost to breast cancer comes in a dream smiling warmly and holding one of her children; a husband who was wasted by a lingering death appears hiking from a mountain side, robust and energetic.

Theologian Rita Nakashima Brock describes such an experience of connection, as well as its power to heal and transform. When her mother died of a painful and disfiguring cancer, Rita says she found herself so depressed that she could barely function at work. One evening she decided to write a letter to her mother in which she poured out her anger for all the wrong things her mother had done to her and for all the hurts she had inflicted. As she raged and wept in the deepest parts of herself, she suddenly found herself writing about all the wonderful things her mother had given her and everything she would miss because she was gone.

Spent with anger and grief, I lay quietly on the floor, eyes open. I felt, more than heard, a wind at the open doorway to the hall and saw my mother, whole and healed, float into the room toward me. Parallel to my body and several feet above it, she looked into my eyes and said, "It's all right."[18]

A peaceful energy returned to Rita, and she knew she was going to be all right.

5. *Creating rituals.* Surviving loss is more difficult in a society which lacks meaningful rituals. Ritual is essential to the grieving process. It allows us to express powerful emotions within the framework some structure provides. Ritual orders the chaos we feel and enables us to mourn with the support of a community. Common sites of mourning allow us to express shared grief. For example, pilgrimages to the Vietnam War Memorial in Washington, D.C., mark a collective sorrow. This monument, with its simply recorded names and dates of the war dead, reminds us of the need for sacramental times and places.

In a number of cultures, older women have a special connection with rites of mourning. Among Native American tribes women were the chief mourners. Loud and prolonged wailing was a manifestation of grief, and though the agonized groans of the bereaved might be sad to hear, they were not considered as painful as silent sorrow. In some tribes, mourning ceremonies in honor of all the dead were part of the yearly religious cycle. Among the Cree, in central Canada, an old woman initiated the celebration. The ceremony began with a distribution of food. Each family that came brought a kettle of food, and after all had eaten, the leader intoned a melancholy song. Everyone joined in the wailing and began a very slow dance, with heads down and shrouded. As each dance finished, another person would start a dirge, and so the dancing continued until morning. The ceremony gave everyone a chance to express their accumulated grief and sadness.[19]

The Christian celebration of All Souls Day offers us a similar opportunity for communal mourning. It arrives on the yearly calendar just as we are witnessing the end of summer and anticipating the coming of winter. Such an annual feast enables us to remember all those who have died, known and unknown. Some communities chant the *Dies Irae* on this day, and have members write out the names of those who have died and place them on the altar where they are kept for the month.[20] Others invite those who have recently lost a loved one to carry the bread and wine forward at the eucharistic liturgy, and to write the names of those who have died in a Book of Life. Among Mexicans and

Mexican-Americans, All Soul's Day is called the day of the dead, el *Día de los Muertos*. It is an occasion to express publicly the many ways the dead are remembered as human beings, and as having arrived at the end of their earthly pilgrimage. In conjunction with All Saints Day, it also provides a time to affirm our belief in the communion of saints, the conviction that we are all—living and dead—joined in one body in Christ. Death is not the end but a transformation to another state of life. One bond unites us in different dimensions of existence and makes soul-to-soul communication possible.

In addition to these communal rituals, we may want to find personal rituals to express the meaning of our loss, especially on anniversaries: lighting a candle in honor of the person, visiting the cemetery. We can also recall what the person valued most—peace, children, the homeless, the environment—and remember them by contributing to these causes in some way.

6. *Staying close to the parables of nature.* I sometimes suggest that a grieving client visit a favorite place in nature and let its parables quietly speak to them. Living, as I do, in the Pacific Northwest, I return in times of sorrow to old growth forests. In the midst of these sacred groves of Douglas firs and western red cedars, western hemlock and Sitka spruce, life and death are inextricably entangled. One of the paradoxes revealed here is that it is the dead trees that are the life of the forest. While the death of a tree is a loss, it is also a vital beginning for the forest ecosystem.[21]

Some trees die upright; others come crashing to the forest floor, toppled by windstorms, landslides, or volcanic flows. The standing dead trees and the fallen ones have different ecological roles. Snags, or standing dead trees, allow many species to escape from predators and harsh weather. Insects and fungi soften the wood, and woodpeckers excavate nesting cavities in snags. Later, other birds and mammals move in. Hollow places in snags are the nesting sites for thirty- to forty-five percent of west-side forest birds; birds such as ospreys and eagles nest in the dead tops of trees.

A decaying log prone on the forest floor reminds us of ancient struggles with storm and disease. From such logs, fresh green branches of hemlocks, spruce, and small plants rise up to catch the afternoon light cutting through giant standing trees. Most western hemlock and many Sitka spruce trees grow from seeds germinated on decomposing nurse logs. It may take centuries for a large log completely to disintegrate; by then the trees rooted in it will have become giants themselves. Rotting snags and logs also provide the cavities needed by black bears, land snails, and other animals; they are the habitat for amazingly diverse mushrooms. Not everything good in the forest comes from its young vigorous growth. New life grows from death, young life and old locked in interdependence.

The silence of these trees creates a kind of cathedral. There is time to meditate on the divine Matrix that gave birth to us, the Divine Wisdom or *Shekinah* in whom we live and move and have our being. We trust this Wisdom to gather up the fragments of our lives, carrying them to new possibilities. Time spent in the forests or gardens of the world will not take away our sorrow. It will, however, allow us to intuit its place in the mystery of all life.

As we age, we know many seasons of mourning. Established systems of meaning shatter. Slowly they are transformed. We learn to love again. An experience I had with a nursing home resident captures for me the hope intrinsic to the grieving process. When I first met her she had just been admitted from the hospital after attempting suicide. She said she was in such great pain one night that she just decided it was too much to bear and was never going to end. So she took all of her pills. Her son found her the next morning and rushed her to the hospital. While we were talking she said that she believed God had forgiven her, but her great sorrow was that she would no longer be able to help others the way she had in the past. She feared her mind and memory were no longer strong enough, damaged by the suicide attempt. She started to recite a favorite poem for me, one that had always sustained her and that described her desire to put love at the center of her life. She began the first lines and then she could remember no more. We both sat for a long time in silence. Finally, I had to leave. Several months later, I met this woman in the cafeteria at lunch time. Much recovered by now, she walked up to me, smiled, and completed the poem.

FOR PRAYER AND REFLECTION

1. Circle of Sorrow

Gather in a circle around a simple table on which are a vase of flowers, a small vessel of oil, and a candle for each person present.

Song and Lighting of Candles

Opening Prayer:

> Restless and yearning, we come before you El Shaddai,
>   our hearts overflowing with sadness.
> Sorrow surges within us; it crashes
>   like waves upon the shore.
> Warm the deep chill within us; abide with us in this
>   bitter season.

Reading: Meanwhile Mary stayed outside near the tomb, weeping. Then, still weeping, she stooped to look inside, and saw two angels in white sitting where the body of Jesus had been, one at the head, the other at the feet. They said, "Woman why are you weeping?" "They have taken my Lord away" she replied "and I don't know where they have put him" (Jn 20:11–14).

Response: (All)

> The bread I eat is ashes,
> My drink is mingled with tears (Ps 102:9).

Sharing of Sorrow: A time of quiet reflection and then each person in the circle shares a sorrow she is mourning, extinguishing her candle as she does so. When the last person is finished, all remain in the silence and darkness for some moments.

Litany *(To be recited antiphonally)*

> Our lives lie in splinters, shards of broken pottery.
> In our suffering we seek you, we hunger, we thirst.
> We cry out in pain, in confusion and sorrow.
> Remember our peoples, our violence-torn nations.
> We mourn for our earth, depleted and ravaged.
> Let not our tears be endless, may our hearts mend and heal.

Anointing: The vessel of oil is passed around the circle, and each in turn takes the hands of the woman next to her, anointing her palms with the oil. As she does so she prays this or a similar blessing: "May our compassionate God bring you healing and comfort."

Readings on God's Mercy (Selections from Julian of Norwich, *Showings*):[22]

Reader 1: And in this he showed me something small, no bigger than a hazelnut, lying in the palm of my hand, and I perceived that it was as round as any ball. I looked at it and thought: What can this be? And I was given the general answer: It is everything which is made. I was amazed that it could last, for I thought that it was so little that it could suddenly fall into nothing. And I was answered in my understanding: It lasts and always will, because God loves it; and thus everything has being through the love of God.

Reader 2: He did not say: You will not be troubled, you will not be belabored, you will not be disquieted; but he said: You will not be overcome.

Reader 3: And this is his intention when he says: You will see yourself that every kind of thing will be well, as if he said: Accept it now in faith and trust, and in the very end you will see truly, in fulness of joy.

Reader 4: And I saw very certainly in this and in everything that before God made us he loved us, which love was never abated and never will be....In this love we have our beginning, and all this shall we see in God without end.

Closing Psalm: (All)

Balance the griefs of our lives with gladness!
Let us see good for as long as we have seen evil.
Reveal the mystery of your designs to us....
Let your beauty and love become plain to our children (Ps 90:14–17).

2. Allowing Grief: A Movement Experience of Lamentation
(designed by D'vorah Kost)

(This can be done alone or in a group. If in a group, make a circle).
     Close your eyes.
     Place crossed hands flat on the center of your chest. Notice the security the top hand gives to the hand underneath. Allow support and comfort to move from your top hand, to the bottom hand, to your heart. Imagine your whole being held in such comforting hands. Allow yourself to soften into the feeling of large imagined hands.
     Tune into the movement of your breath in your chest. Deepen it slightly. Let your spine softly rock or undulate with the rhythm and direction of your breath.

Tune into your emotions, thoughts, memories, dreams come and gone. Let your thoughts and feelings sway you. Relax your neck, let your head hang and move from side to side. Time of sounding: sighing, weeping, crying, wailing, if so moved.

After the sounds quiet, focus on the aspect of grief that implies transformation. After fully grieving over time, one is never quite the same as before. Going fully into grief can give rise to rebirth. Ask the question: "What can now come forth?"

Now let the back of the right hand rest firmly in the palm of the left. Wrap your left fingers around your thumb palm so that you can see your fingernails. Fold the fingers of your right hand so that the tips just cover your left fingernails. See a tree in the shape and lines that your fingers make.

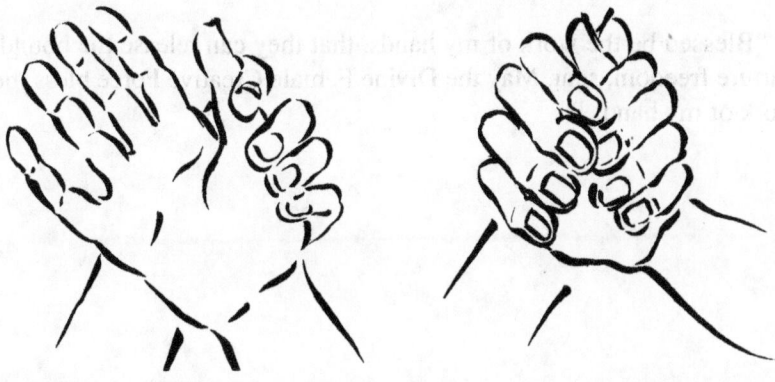

Place it against your heart and feel the strength in that connection. Be with the tree imagery and symbolism. "Blessed be the work of my hands, that they can be strong, can give strength, provide sustenance."

Unfold your fingers, hook your thumbs and spread your fingers as wings. Stretch your fingers and palms to their limit. Feel the release from bound to free. Let your fingers and hands express a bird in flight.

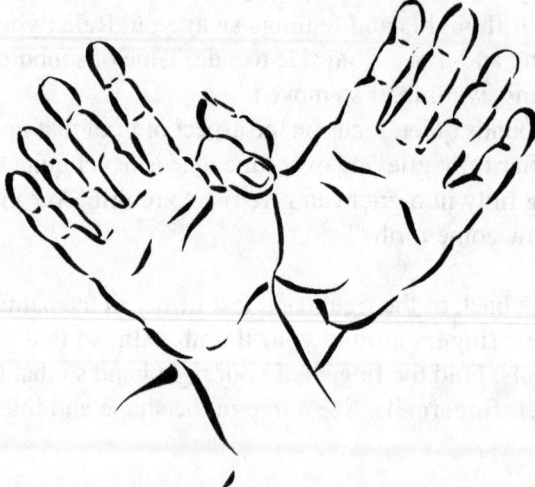

"Blessed be the work of my hands, that they can release the bound, nurture freedom, soar. May the Divine Female Creative Force bless the work of my hands."

Chapter 7

Remembrance and Redemption

> And Mary stored up all these things in her heart, pondering them (Lk 52:2).

To celebrate her sixtieth birthday, a friend was invited on a family cruise. What happened when they set sail surprised her. She was on deck waving to well-wishers along the shore as the ship pulled away from land. The crowd on the dock turned to go, and suddenly the sight of their backs triggered an old buried memory. She was once again a young woman of eighteen, standing at the rail of a ship headed from Europe to America. She watched her parents turn and leave as the vessel moved out to sea. They were sending her to safety as the winds of war began to envelop Europe. Now for the first time, so many years later, she wept the tears of that painful parting.

All that we have been and done continues to live on as part of us. Our history dwells in our whole being. In Margaret Laurence's *The Stone Angel*, Hagar says of herself at ninety-two: "Now I am rampant with memory."[1] When she was eighty-three, Elizabeth Coatsworth wrote in *Personal Geography: Almost an Autobiography*:

> I like this sense that all my life and experience is contained in me. I am a five-year-old child in Egypt, I am a schoolgirl in a very strict private school on Park Street in Buffalo, I roam the beaches of Lake Erie, barefoot all summer....[2]

All these things and a thousand more, she says, are embodied in her. Coatsworth muses that although outwardly she is eighty-three, inwardly she is every age, with all the emotions and experiences of each of these periods. As the years accumulate, we revisit earlier memories for many reasons. Even our treatment of ourselves as adults, whether gentle or demanding, is a way of remembering how we were once treated. Past realities pass through our minds and hearts again, shaping identity and self-understanding. Memory is a source of surprising new discoveries and entrenched convictions. It is a reservoir of both joy and anguish. The past shapes the present in powerful ways.

Christians are a community based on deep remembering or *anamnesis*. In the eucharist we break the bread and drink the wine as Jesus asked us: "Do this in memory of me." In symbolic action we make present the power of Jesus' death and resurrection. Remembrance becomes redemption. This is meant to be the pattern of all our remembering: experiencing the moments of our lives not only as past time, but as sacred time; finding in the stories of our lives the story of God.

This is not always easily done. When we remember, we not only recall facts; we invest them with particular meanings. Remembrance is an act of the imagination, a reconfiguring of events. We screen past events through a lens or filter and reinterpret them. Recollection of the past can produce satisfaction and joy. But as one woman remarked, our lens is not always "a lens of forgiveness." The past may appear as a series of failures or tragedies, its tattered pieces hard to patch together. Others have let us down, and we have disappointed ourselves. Viewing our lives through certain glasses, it is possible to become stuck, hardened, and despondent.

If memory is to be a graced experience, we may need new lenses. These are present for us in the way Jesus responds to women in the gospels. He reveals to us the eye of God, and asks us to view our lives in a similar way. This, he says, is how we are to remember—we are to let our lives pass through the compassionate heart of God. A woman is accused of adultery (Jn 8:2–11). Jesus refuses to join in the condemnations and judgments; instead he offers her forgiveness. No stones are thrown, and she can stop hurling them at herself. A woman who has suffered an incurable flow of blood for twelve years touches Jesus and taps into power and healing. She at last finds peace and freedom (Mk 5:25–34). Mary Magdalene is a true and steadfast friend to Jesus during his ministry, sufferings, and death. Her future role honors that past. She is the first disciple to see the risen Jesus, and the first sent to preach the good news of the resurrection (Jn 20:1–18). In contrast to the judgment and despair through which we often filter our memories, women in the gospels are offered forgiveness, wholeness, joy, and possibility. This gospel perspective enables us to find redemption even in painful memories.

Viewing Our Lives with Compassion

We instinctively evaluate our lives. Sometimes there is a partially formulated question that guides the process: How well have I used my gifts? Have I been a good wife and mother? Have I come close at all to being what God had in mind in creating me? A mother is telling me about her adult son's recent arrest on a drug charge. Her struggle with this news takes her back to her first years with him. She recalls her joy at his birth, the initial happiness, the time when things changed, and the troubled years that followed. This remembering is an evaluation of herself as a mother: Did she love him well enough? What difference did it make that she was ill for part of those years? She sorts through these events over and over again. Reviewing them can take her to many different places.

One of the prospects we most fear about aging is becoming mired in bitterness and resentment. It is possible to age in such a way that we become stuck in cynicism. As the years of our lives pile up, their remainder is like the stale grounds of coffee that remain long after breakfast is over.

> I resented my own decision to retire when I did. I said, "Why'd I ever do that?" I was hating myself. One can be consumed with remorse at wrong turnings made, at failures and all kinds of things where one wished one had lived differently. I have gone through agonies of soul-searching, seeking not only forgiveness, but self-forgiveness.[3]

As in this woman's experience, the residue is often what we have been unable to accept in ourselves.

While working with women in therapy and spiritual direction, I hear the many voices that live inside them. There is a voice that knows what they most value and what direction they would like to take. It is sometimes fragile and tentative, hard to hear amid the din of other messages. Then there are other voices that critique and judge this voice. Their language is peppered with shoulds and oughts; it lacks compassion: "Look at what your other women friends have accomplished during their lifetimes; they are creative and productive and you've really done very little of value." Margaret, for example, who is in her mid-fifties, can never remember a time when she was free of these competing voices. She is bright and attractive, but tormented by doubts about herself whenever she undertakes a project in the law firm where she works. Ultimately these voices

seem to her to be the way God views her: she will be judged and found
wanting unless she uses her talents to the full. She cannot seem to find an
emotional place where God's compassion could be a part of her life.

One woman said that in her forties, she became aware of how negative an influence ideals had been in her life: "I've been thinking about
ideals and how I used them—mostly to beat myself up. I don't think I
ever saw them as something I could become—only what I should be
and am not." As we age we become more aware of those dark places in
ourselves that seem impervious to change. There is an enemy within,
different for each of us. We become familiar with the divided human
heart—our own and others. Now in her late seventies, a mother and
grandmother formulates her key spiritual struggle:

> Why do I always have to be right? What I want before I die is to
> learn how to love, to let go of the sharpness and the closed heart
> that frighten others and distance them from me. I see it in myself
> back across the years and, if anything, it is stronger than ever
> now—when I most want to be free of it.

At the heart of her pain is the awareness that she has tried for years to
remedy this, to no avail: "I am old enough to know that I have been like
this for a long, long time." Something different is needed.

Embracing the darkness is, paradoxically, a path to healing it.
Throughout life we can carry with us an image of perfection, a self that
will some day be free of what troubles and limits us. If we only work hard
enough at it, we can eliminate it. Substituting a model of wholeness for
perfection allows us to take it in as part of ourselves. The darkness takes
on a different feel. Darkness and light become two poles of the self that
we begin at mid-life to embrace. Then they turn to us, in various ways, a
new face. What looked like light may turn out to be darkness, and what
looked like darkness, light.

The capacity to embrace these aspects of the self begins in openness
to the love of God. If we can believe we are loved by the divine,
embraced by the compassionate womb of God, we can perhaps hold all
of ourselves as sacred. At times it is harder to live with happiness and
joy than it is to deal with suffering, harder to believe that it is what God
wants for us. In doing therapy I am often struck by how unfamiliar and
even uncomfortable some women find happiness. It is hard to believe
in the joy, to think it is what they are meant to know. Ultimately this has
to do with how we see God.

Forgiving Self and Others

Looking at our lives we discover not only mistakes we have made, but hurts we have received. These give rise to anger, blame, and help-lessness. We may be preoccupied with the injury, with fantasies of revenge, with conflict that it seems will never end. These feelings may be accompanied by an inner sense that we *should* forgive, but a con-viction that we are unable to do so: "I wonder if I will ever be able to forgive him." "I keep telling myself: call her up; and let go of this. But I simply can't bring myself to do it." The actions of another have brought about a fundamental change in our lives and the person needs to know and be punished. We feel turmoil and unrest. We may try to forgive, only to find the pain and anger rising again.

Forgiveness has two dimensions. It includes the experience of being forgiven, as well as that of forgiving others. Neither is a simple act of the will. Each is a long and complex process of healing. Being forgiven brings about a fundamental shift in our way of being in the world.[4] Before this there is often a growing awareness that something is wrong, a sense of estrangement from self and others. This alienation is a result of broken connections; we long to be in relationship again with God, self, and others. Forgiveness restores us to the world; we feel once again at home. It also changes our relationship to the past—that is, to ourselves—and gives us a new future.

In her writings on old age, Helen Luke says that the ultimate free-dom of spirit comes only with this breakthrough of forgiveness. Through the *metanoia* which is a gift of the Spirit, a transformation takes place, and we enter into the meaning of incarnation. We let go of every false guilt—whether seen as our own or another's—and accept the real guilt each of us carries, our refusal to see and be aware. Luke believes we can then look open-eyed at ourselves and the world, and know both the joy and the pain of the human condition. We hold all our weaknesses and other injustices and injuries in the darkness that reveals the light, as "notes in the music of God."[5]

In being forgiven and forgiving, we are once again restored to the human community. We no longer need to deny our limitations, failings, and dependence on others. Through a kind of grieving process, we let go of former ways of viewing ourselves and others. We experience a longing for what might have been and will never be, regret at the harm we have caused. We find that we are more like, than different from, those who have hurt us; we, too, can become enraged, and can be hurtful.[6] We now accept what we previously had to negate in ourselves. This is different from being weighed down by a sense of shame and guilt; in fact, it frees us from those burdens. The experience of being forgiven by God and others restores a fundamental sense of acceptance and worth.

Forgiveness of others flows from forgiveness of self. As an interpersonal reality, it is affected by every aspect of the relationship: the strength of the bond, the history of trust, the admission of guilt by the person who has wronged us. The process of forgiveness is hard to describe because it takes as many twists and turns as an individual life. Understanding the meaning of an injury in our lives takes time and includes many levels of insight into our pain and the meaning of letting go. It is a layered process, and does not have to be total to be helpful. Forgiveness does not mean that we overlook offenses and pretend they never happened; nor that we give up protection of self. We need only begin the process, be open to healing, and pray for the grace of forgiveness; the rest will come. One therapist suggests four stages of forgiveness: to forgo (leave it alone), to forbear (to abstain from punishing), to forget (to avert from memory, to refuse to dwell), to forgive (to abandon the debt).[7] She stresses that our part in the process is to refuse to dwell, to punish, to recollect. We stop bringing up the wrong again and again, and make a conscious decision not to hold resentment and retaliate.

Forgiveness of another paradoxically frees us from their power to determine our lives. As long as our energy is absorbed in hatred and resentment, it is unavailable to us for other things. Forgiveness restores us to our selves; we can center on our own desires and live out of them. A burden lifts and energy flows again. We can reclaim parts of ourselves that were blocked by the injury: our sexuality, our freedom of expression, our gifts of joy and laughter. Forgiveness enlarges our sense of ourselves and the possibilities available in life. In one of her poems, Alice Walker captures the complex dimensions of this reality.

> Looking down into my father's
> dead face
> for the last time
> my mother said without
> tears, without smiles
> without regrets
> but with *civility*
> "Goodnight, Willie Lee, I'll see you
> in the morning."

> And it was then I knew that the healing
> of all our wounds
> is forgiveness
> that permits a promise
> of our return
> at the end.[8]

To forgive and be forgiven both enables us to live and prepares us to die.

The experience of any kind of forgiveness is a cycle of judgment and acceptance, refusal and outreach. As we make our way through this cycle, it is important to experience the acceptance of others. Those who listen to us and receive without judgment and in love the parts of us that we want to reject—our hatred, mistakes, ignorance, capacity to hurt others, hardness, anger—restore us to ourselves. They embody for us God's loving acceptance. When others can know these places and not reject us, we find that we can reconnect with those parts ourselves. That is also why it is so painful when we are not forgiven by another; we experience a connection being withheld, and are powerless to do anything about it.

Because forgiveness is so often misused as motivation in women's lives, it is important to be clear about what it is *not*. It is not the absence of boundaries and limits. Psychological and spiritual reconciliation with another does not imply that face-to-face reconciliation will or should occur. In fact, forgiveness may restore a necessary sense of separateness within a relationship. When we can face fully the potential for harm in another and in the universe, we are free to let go of certain relationships. The most appropriate way to honor what we now know about a person and a relationship may be to have no further contact whatsoever with them. This is often the case in situations of abuse, battering, and assault. Forgiveness does not mean putting ourselves in harm's way. It includes a realistic appreciation of the potential for evil in ourselves and others.

Certain memories have a quality that differs from our other remembering.[9] They may feel like a lifetime of grief. They may evoke a terror or sadness that feels too large to hold by ourselves. These are traumatic memories. In the fourth and fifth decades of life, many women are strong and free enough to work at healing earlier trauma. This remembering may be precipitated by a life event such as the breakup of a marriage or the illness or death of a parent. Many survivors of abuse reach adulthood with their secrets still held in silence. Traumatic memories often lack verbal narrative and are held as vivid images and bodily sensations.

Some of these come from childhood experiences; they may also be later events of rape or battering. The power and pain of such memories is such that we must be certain we have a safe holding place before attempting to deal with them. Usually this is a counseling setting of some kind where a trained professional can help us move through the experience.

Though we can open ourselves to it and prepare for it, forgiveness of any kind comes finally as a grace. We may be aware of a turning point in a dream or a moment of prayer. Resolution frequently comes in moments of harmony deeper than reason. A woman tells how she experienced it:

> It had been raining that day, there was a beautiful rainbow that stretched from one side of that valley to the other. So I just pulled up on the rest area up on top of the hill there and just parked the car and just took it all in. It was as though that was God's covenant with me, that, yes, all the struggles we've gone through are OK and you're going to make it.[10]

This grace of forgiveness comes not once, but at many points throughout the process.

Through forgiveness we experience ourselves as held in a love that can embrace all that we are; this offers us the opportunity to embrace it as well. In the final pages of her novel, *Little Altars Everywhere*, Rebecca Wells closes her account of a family struggling with decades of pain. Earlier in the novel we learn of the suffering brought by alcoholism and physical and sexual abuse. Now the daughter, Siddalee, describes how the sense of being held by a larger presence has become a part of her healing. She remembers a Christmas when her Daddy bought the whole family cowgirl and cowboy outfits and they wore them to mass at Our Lady of Divine Compassion church. She remembers walking up to the communion rail in her orange cowgirl skirt, shirt, hat, and boots, opening her mouth to receive the body and blood of Jesus and knowing for a moment what it meant to be pure, true, clean and unashamed. She remembers believing that the reason everyone was staring at her family was that they were so magnificent, believing for that moment that everything would be fine—not perfect, but fine.

> On good days now, I can feel that way for hours. Feel like there is a big pair of hands holding me up. Feel like underneath the terror there is some kind of wonder waiting for me. And sometimes I

believe what I knew for a split second on that Christmas morning: that the mother who holds me isn't Mama. She's somebody bigger, somebody much older, somebody so tender that just looking into her eyes is like a sweet, much needed nap. She speaks to me daily, this mother, with little private signs. And all I have to do is keep walking, with my ears tuned and my eyes wide open."[11]

This is Siddalee's experience of the mystery in whom we "live and move and have our being" (Acts 17:28). In this embrace, her suffering somehow becomes a kind of love.

As a child Siddalee had thought that the whole world looked like little altars everywhere, that all things and people in their everyday lives had holy sparks in them. Her sacramental vision now takes on the measure of all the suffering she has known since those childhood days. When, as an adult, she returns to Thornton, Louisiana, for the baptism of her goddaughter, she experiences forgiveness and a sense again of connection with the universe. In the sacrament of that moment her family stands in a circle around Siddalee and she feels their breathing as also the breathing of parched babies in drought-stricken lands, as part of one giant bellows. She realizes that she cannot save her family nor lead them out of darkness. All she can do is hold them, love them, not hurt them, not close her heart. And that is enough.

Claiming the Events of Our Lives

Memory is a way of connecting. As we move through life, we are continually involved in a process of finding meaning in the present by reinterpreting the past. We reassemble lost parts of ourselves. Virginia Woolf calls memory a seamstress who runs "her needle in and out, up and down, hither and thither."[12] This joining of past and present is the narrative thread that supports our identity. Reminiscing helps us to maintain a sense of self. It is one of the reasons why women often turn to the past when life transitions raise anew the questions: Who am I? What is my life all about? The past takes on new meaning in response to present questions and needs. Research suggests that such reminiscence inclines toward sharing and mutuality.[13] It goes best in the company of others. In sharing our stories with others, we come to understand them ourselves. The metaphor of a sewing or quilting circle suggests the way in which support from others enables us to find and connect the threads of our identity.

Memory is about time, and women's time is cyclical. Our stories show less a pattern of linear movement toward one clear goal than a repetitive, cumulative structure. Through reminiscence, or thinking and talking about the past, we may come upon something we have known all our lives, but now understand in a new way. Beginning to play the piano again after many years, a woman discovers a stream of images, each, as it were, connected to notes of the piece she is playing. Her life seems to become hers again as she plays. A woman who used painting as a form of life review called one of her works, "Puzzle Bottle." This print, she said, could be thought of as her life, a puzzle she was trying to assemble to give structure to chaotic experience.

> I think my life has been like a puzzle, a sort of mixed up kind of life. There are things in my life that really confused me. I think workin' at this art has helped me to bring it all together where I feel more complete, more at peace with myself for things that happened way back years ago.[14]

For her, art was a means of synthesizing past experiences with current self-image. It was a powerful tool, she said, because "it helps you put it outside yourself."

Memories have other memories inside and between them. They are complex and layered realities. We circle back again to the same stories, hoping to finally make sense of these fragments within the whole. We repeat stories hoping in some way to escape from the repetition.

> But if you can find a way to penetrate the surface of those experiences and start to discern the pattern, find the meaning in the pattern—the sort of crazy quilt of your life—then you transform your life into a work of art and understand that the most horrible experiences are the biggest learning tools.[15]

In the process of remembering, we create a new story. The image of quilting captures this well. How can we stitch together the pieces of our lives so that some fresh pattern or meaning emerges? Pondering the meaning of life, what we get are not always great revelations, but "little daily miracles, illuminations, matches struck unexpectedly in the dark."[16]

We are continually recomposing our lives. We do so when we experience a major loss, at times of surgery or illness, when we move to a new location. This may become more intense in the middle years of a woman's life when she senses a disjunction between her present reality and the narratives she has used to explain how she got there. Marriage no longer seems what she thought it was; the ideal family does not exist. Kate Armstrong in Margaret Drabble's novel, *The Middle Ground*, expresses it this way:

> I no longer trust my own memories....I thought they made sense, that there was a clear pattern, but maybe I've got it all wrong, maybe there's some other darker pattern, entirely different.[17]

Such times of crisis provide an opening for a larger and fuller look at the past, a chance to incorporate new elements into a too simple view. This loss of an idealized self can be frightening at first, but it is also freeing. The identity that emerges is larger and more complete, more attuned to the realities of past, present, and future.

Claiming the events of our lives includes attending to the joy. God dwells within our personal histories. But this becomes clear only if we stop to notice. As we age, we find ourselves listening to our lives as a whole. We attend to whatever of holiness we find there. There are moments of sacredness, times of revelation. We pray out of our lives. At my sister's wedding, my husband and I were walking with my mother on the beach. As she reflected on her recovery from several serious illnesses, her prayer was spontaneous. She probably did not even think of it as a prayer: "Whenever I needed it, God gave me strength. He helped me get well enough to be at this wedding." Another woman describes this sense of celebration of her life as she reaches middle age:

> All my sins, errors, my most serious mistakes are part of the whole and do not, when my thought is so huge, cancel out the other emotions—of love, and above all else, of gratitude for having been born at all.[18]

Memory allows us to feel positive emotions again, to return to events that bring pleasure and fullness: the fun of family trips to the ocean, the laughter of children celebrating a birthday, the warm embrace of a beloved friend, the yellow of rose bushes edging a house, the fragrance of lilacs shifting in the breeze. Reminiscing is often a sensory experience.[19] We hear the melodies again of a favorite tune; we smell the chili simmering in the kitchen; we see the face of our son as he arrives home.

These may be fragmentary and fleeting, but our senses hold some of our happiest moments. They continue to live in us as vessels of grace and renewal, and returning to them is a form of spiritual enrichment.

Moments of personal integration can happen when memories stored in the body are triggered by ritual. Anthropologist Barbara Myerhoff describes such an experience in *Number Our Days*, her moving portrayal of Jewish old people in Venice, California. The Sabbath was celebrated at the Aliyah Senior Citizens' Center on Fridays. On this day Basha, one of the members, was called to light the candles and say the blessing. This candle blessing was a powerful event during which she experienced a unification with her mother and with herself as a child. After the service she asked if others knew what it meant to her. Then she proceeded to tell them that as a little girl she had stood beside her mother when she lit the candles for Shabbat. They were alone in the house, with everything warm and quiet, the good smells of cooking all around.

> My braids very tight, to last through Shabbes, made with my best ribbons. Whatever we had, we wore our best. To this day, when the heat of the candles is on my face, I circle the flame and cover my eyes, and then I feel again my mother's hands on my smooth cheeks.[20]

Often a ritual or devotion preserves intact the original context in which we have experienced it. Its symbols gather up an accumulation of gestures, sounds, feelings, and historical moments. As Myerhoff says, these are rooted in the deepest layers of our hearts. Depending on the way we come to experience these layers, we either find changes in the rituals very difficult, or reject them altogether.

As we age we also experience nostalgia. Nostalgia differs from memory in that it is a kind of forgetting. In nostalgia we edit out the unpleasant and painful details, the anger, anxiety, impatience, and fatigue. Nostalgia is a desire to return home again, to capture a time when we were happy. For example, it is Christmas, and a mother tells me that it will never be what Christmas was when her children were small and they were all home together. She remembers the tree and lights, the gifts and delight. Edited out are the exhaustion and disappointment, the irritation and quarreling. Memory usually does not let us separate out the pain so fully. At a retreat on spirituality and aging, I once asked participants to return to a time in which they had felt loved, to a joyful memory. Many in the group had a similar experience: joy and sorrow were inextricably intertwined. One person recalled the happiness of her fiftieth wedding anniversary, only to find the memory filled with the pain of her husband's recent death. Another tapped into the energy of a treasured friendship, but uncovered hidden hurts and lapses in caring as well.

The attempt to bring past moments into a coherent pattern is sometimes called life review. Since it is a path to meaning, it is also a preparation for death. Florida Scott Maxwell says it best:

> You need only claim the events of your life to make yourself yours. When you truly possess all you have been and done, which may take some time, you are fierce with reality. When at last age has assembled you together, will it not be easy to let it all go, lived, balanced, over?[21]

Such descriptions of life review may give the impression that lives can be perfectly resolved. But the process of integration remains incomplete. We have only a provisional understanding. This allows us to be ever open to the reshaping of our stories, to new discoveries. This remains true up to the very end of our lives. New dreams and fresh directions emerge as we balance past, present, and future; as we integrate light and darkness, unconscious and conscious elements in our lives. Since our stories are also sacred stories, their unfinished quality leaves room for the redemption that God is bringing about in us and in all of creation.

Creating a Future

We remember the past in order to reimage the future. For clues to where we are going, we search for where we have been. In this way, memory is about choice and change.

Endings are often a return to the beginning. Memory allows us to capture lost aspects of ourselves, to retrieve an original self perhaps buried for years. First we feel the gap between potential—who we once were and wanted to be—and what we have become. We recall the young girl whose strengths and aspirations got lost on the way to adult life. Perhaps this girl believed she could write, but her poems and stories were silenced by a critic or by the demands of life. As one woman approached her fiftieth birthday, she was flooded with images of herself as a young girl in Sunday school, enthralled by the Bible stories that the teacher told. She had not read scripture for a long time, but she sensed that a deeply important part of her spirituality was held by that little girl, and she began tentatively to approach the Bible again. Other women remember always wanting to be a priest, and this memory fuels their determination to open all ministries to women and to provide their own daughters and granddaughters with symbolism of women as sacred. We realize with pain how our gifts and futures were restricted by the religious and cultural definitions of what we could be as women. We may have spent many years living out a role that did not suit us at all. To forget this is to risk losing the chance to create something different for ourselves and other women who follow us.

Meaning always lives in a specific cultural tradition and historical context. Our personal memories are held in the context of larger events. A powerful work of the imagination which explores the role of memory and story in the liberation of her people is Toni Morrison's novel, *Beloved*. She dedicates the novel to the black and angry dead, the sixty million and more victims of the diaspora. The past behind the action of *Beloved* is a people decimated by slavery, a world in which "anybody (you) knew, let alone loved, who hadn't run off or been hanged, got rented out, loaned out, bought up, brought back, stored up, mortgaged, won, stolen or seized." In such a world you "protected yourself and loved small."[22] In *Beloved* we witness the effort to love and trust again, to find the connections that make it possible to go on. At first the characters are determined to forget. But the refusal to confront the pain of the past keeps it continually alive. In *Beloved* Morrison shows the link between trust and remembering: the past is most healing when it is remembered and told in response to the needs of another. Remembering and telling are a kind of loving, feeding, nurturing, and creating. By memory and narration we rebuild our world.

Morrison coins a word for the kind of delving into the past that leads to a transformed future; she describes it as "rememory." This kind of remembrance of suffering is sometimes called "dangerous memory" because it leads to action to reverse oppression. Such memory not only keeps alive the suffering and hopes of the past, but creates new horizons. It is the kind of recollection that leads to visions such as Mary's *Magnificat*, her great song of liberation. In it Mary praises God's action on behalf of all oppressed people, and proclaims her confidence in the divine promise of a transformed social order. She evokes the powerful memory of God's redemption throughout history: "God's mercy reaches from age to age" (Lk 1:50). Through the years of storing up all these things in her heart, Mary came to know how God remembers us. She knew that it is this divine remembrance that finally redeems our own remembering.

1. Praying the Joyful and Sorrowful Mysteries of Our Lives. (This is designed to be prayed with a group, but could also be used for personal prayer.)

Opening Instrumental Music and Time of Silent Reflection:

What moments of your life stand out in strongest detail in your memory? What voices and faces from your past are most vivid? What emotions do they evoke in you?

What are the scenes of some of your deepest joys and greatest sadnesses? What graces have come to you from each?

What decisions made you happiest, and which do you most regret? Have you found a way to let go of the mistakes and failures?

Litany: A litany is a gathering of memories. We bring our own recollections and share in those of others. This litany recalls both joyful and sorrowful moments of our lives.

Sorrowful Memories: (Response: Forgive us, we pray.)
For failing to risk...
For hardness of heart...
For refusing to listen...
For doubting our gifts...
(Add your own.)

Painful Memories: (Response: Show us your love.)
When sadness fills our hearts...
When we recall senseless tragedy...
When losses sear us anew...
When we are reminded of past pain...
(Add your own.)

Joyful Memories: (Response: We give you thanks.)
For strength in the hard times...
For love of family and friends...
For times of joy and laughter...

For the beauty of life…
(Add your own.)

Closing Prayer:
Shekinah, El Shaddai, abiding with us
   each moment of our lives,
   you have promised that though others forget us,
   you will cherish and remember us,
   and redeem our days.
You who weep with us in our pain
   and rejoice with us in our happiness,
   be with us in our remembering,
   that we may see our past
   as it is seen by your compassionate love.
   Amen.

2. Ritual for Moving from a Home of Many Years

Gather in the entry to the home. The person or persons moving from the home or someone designated by them carries a lighted candle. Another person brings a basket and/or scrapbook in which to store memories from each room. You may also wish to use an audio or video tape to record memories.

Opening Refrain (repeated in full at beginning; then the first lines only recited in each room):

"I will set up my dwelling among you, and I will not desert you. I will live in your midst; I will be your God and you shall be my people.

It is I, your God, who have brought you out of the land of Egypt. I have broken the yoke that bound you and have made you walk with head held high" (Lev 26:11–13).

The group moves from room to room of the home. The following ritual is repeated in each:

—Upon entering each room light a candle which has been placed there.

—Share stories of the happy and sad times experienced in that room.

—The person leaving the home is given a symbol of this room to take to her next home, e.g., pictures for a scrapbook, a small momento which is placed in her basket of memories, written memories of special times there.

—The person taking leave blows out the candle. While leaving the room, all recite together the refrain: "I will set up my dwelling among you, and I will not desert you. I will live in your midst; I will be your God and you shall be my people."

Prayer (upon returning to starting place):
You, O God, have been our dwelling place from age to age,
> we ask you to heal the sad and painful events that took place in this house. Bring to us the winnowing fan of your mercy that separates wheat from chaff. Show us how to save what can be saved and to let the rest go.

You who meet us in the places and people with whom we live,
> we give thanks for the growth and the joy we have found in this home. We know we stand on holy ground. Your presence glances off furniture and walls, tables and shelves. As we say goodbye, may we carry with us the blessings lived in every room.

Celebration and Refreshments

Chapter 8

Giving and Receiving Care

> Whatever I do in life, whomever I meet,
> I am first and always one-caring or
> one cared-for.
> —Nel Noddings, *Caring*[1]

Several years ago I worked at a center in downtown Seattle where older residents of the area could come for lunch and other activities. In one of my groups was Julie, a woman in her late eighties whose quiet presence always seemed to anchor our discussions. If someone felt they had nothing to say, she would protest: "Oh, no, I simply don't believe there isn't one thing of interest in all your days," and then she would listen with rapt attention as the person began to decide that maybe there was this one area they "hadn't thought to tell us about." The rest of the group began to take new notice of the person as well.

One November Julie asked me if I would do something for her. She said she wanted me to help her up the incline outside the center's front door to the level sidewalk just above it. The rise had become too steep for her to manage alone. I took her arm and as we arrived at the top, she turned and said: "Thank you, I can make it fine now." She moved into the crowded street, looking defenseless against the rain and late autumn darkness settling over the city. Her cotton dress and sweater seemed little protection, and I wanted to run after her to offer her more help, to advise her to wear a coat, to warn her of possible dangers lurking in the darkness. But she had told me exactly what she needed and asked me to let her walk the rest of the way on her own.

I have been a part of many caregiving situations since that time, and some of them have involved agonizing decisions and painful confrontations with suffering and death. Yet when I ponder the spirituality of caregiving, Julie always comes to mind. I think that is because she understood so clearly that caregiving is not a one-directional flow of energy, not simply giving to or doing for another who is in need. She challenged me to respond to her need but leave her free, to see caregiving as an exchange of gifts, a mutual sharing of frailty and strengths.

What does it mean to care and to be cared for? The sharing of care raises fundamental spiritual issues for women, especially as we enter the second half of life. Each of us who lives long enough will know it in many forms. We care for children, parents, friends, a spouse, or brothers and sisters. We ourselves experience conditions that leave us weak and dependent on others for even the most basic tasks. Moving through these experiences we touch the meaning of Christian love in all its breadth and details.

A spirituality of care is a tough, earthy spirituality. In the concreteness of giving and receiving care we live out the gospel injunction to love both ourselves and others well. We experience and mediate Christ's love. This is made clear in chapters 13–17 of John's gospel, Jesus' farewell discourse.[2] Speaking to his disciples just before his arrest, trial, and death, Jesus offers a vision of the new life possible for his followers. At the heart of this vision is the community's love for one another. By this love the community will continue the work and presence of Jesus after his death and resurrection.

> I give you a new commandment, that you love one another. Just as I have loved you, you should love one another. By this love you have for one another, everyone will know that you are my disciples (13:34–35).

Experience tells us that loving one another may be the most difficult thing Jesus asks of us. But the language of love found in John is a language of fullness rather than emptiness. In this it differs from the language of discipleship found in the synoptic gospels. According to John's account, we give our lives for our friends as an act of love, not as an act of self-denial and sacrifice. This emphasis on the fullness and abundance of love is especially important for women; stress on emptying and self-denial has led many women to set aside the needs of the self and embrace an ideal of endless self-sacrifice.

Living the gospel means finding ways to maintain and enhance this mutual caring that flows from the fullness of love. Five are suggested here: listening to our emotions, acknowledging the limits of care, receiving the gifts of care, finding the balance in caring, and widening the circle of support.

Listening to Our Emotions

In light of the numerous tasks and practical decisions intrinsic to situations of care, emotions may seem like luxury items. But studies indicate that it is not the physical demands of caring for someone that are most burdensome; it is the breakdown in meaningful personal interaction. The core issue is what we do with what we feel. We may deny our feelings, but they will seep out in indirect ways. Paradoxically, the more we are able to tolerate a range of feelings in ourselves, the more responsive we can be to others. A narrowing of what we will allow as appropriate feeling in ourselves also limits our ability to respond to another's emotions. Further, dealing with the emotional aspects of a caregiving situation is intrinsic to the process of physical healing. Emotions are never purely mental or purely physical. They are always an expression of our mind/body unity, essentially psychosomatic events.

Emotions carry insight and knowledge. They also carry energy. Positive uses of this energy can release creativity and open new levels of communication; energy that is ignored turns to acid, burning ever deeper into body and spirit. In *Theaters of the Body*, psychoanalyst Joyce McDougall reminds us that when our conflicts and psychic pain have no other outlets, our other organs—the heart, the stomach, the lungs—express the pain or sorrow.[3] We try to communicate an emotional experience through organic illness. We may be unable to recognize or tolerate what we are feeling, but our bodies cry out in despair. This may also give us access to the human expressions of care that we cannot find in any other way.

Physical illness is related to emotional distress in many ways. There are the addictions, those ways of using alcohol, drugs, food, or other behavior to deal with distressing conflicts by temporarily blurring the awareness of their existence. They are ineffective, however, in permanently dealing with the pain, so we repeat the behavior again and again. McDougall believes that we all use action rather than reflection when our usual defenses against emotional pain are overwhelmed. Instead of becoming aware that we are feeling guilty, anxious, or angry, we overeat, quarrel with a friend, have an accident, or come down with a cold. These are examples of what she calls "expression in action," ways in which we disperse emotion rather than thinking about the precipitating event and the feelings connected with it.

One way out of this cycle is greater awareness of what we are feeling and why. Experiences of giving and receiving care generate powerful emotions. It is helpful to name and learn from them. This means acknowledging our needs and vulnerabilities and not being ashamed of them: "Real pain is there, and if we have to be falsely cheerful, it is part of our isolation."[4] We need to know that we have every right to feel angry, confused, or sad. We accept as part of ourselves our jealousy, smallness, or reluctance. We are not surprised to find contradictory emotions within ourselves: appreciation for the help we are given and resentment at having to ask for it, anger with a loved one and pity for the person who suffers so deeply. But if we can hear what is within us, our actions and decisions will take account of all that is there. The negative emotions—anger, guilt, hatred, helplessness—are most difficult to bear. It helps when they can be shared—within the caregiving situation itself, when possible—or with a friend, pastor, counselor, or support group. In this sharing we learn that others also do things imperfectly, lose patience, feel guilty. This is healing knowledge.

Caregivers describe many common emotions. There is often guilt. We cannot meet the ideal of what care could be. We fail to do all that the person we are caring for wants or needs. Our actions may bring about results we did not intend. All of this causes conflict and guilt. We may also feel guilt that we have been spared the suffering the one we are caring for has to endure. When I am talking to my mother and she is having a bad day and tells me so, I sense an unease growing in me. It is hard simply to listen to her account without translating it into an indictment of the quality and extent of my caring: Should I be there to see her more often? Am I doing enough? Is she blaming me?

We stand empty-handed and powerless in the face of suffering, loss, and pain. Sharing another's pain when we can do nothing about it is very costly. We feel sadness and helplessness. Sometimes we want to run away. Life can be unfair and cruel, and it is excruciating to stand by, unable to do anything. The ability to do something—almost anything— helps us deal with the pain, and that is why even offering someone a drink of water is a relief. But sometimes there is literally nothing we can do.

When we feel helpless, our temptation is to try to rescue, give advice, or explain away the pain and frustration. It is much more difficult to acknowledge the helplessness. Prayer is often a way of expressing it. We cup the person in our empty hands, lifting them in their pain and woundedness up to God, often not knowing exactly what it is we are asking in our prayer. Sending the person healing energy, love, and prayer allows God to embrace us all in our pain. It is also sustaining to remember the power of presence. More important than what we *do* for others is the way in which we *are* with them. What we most need from one another, both the one caring and the one cared for, is companionship, the willingness to walk together into the darkness. During a time of caregiving a friend wrote me: "We never feel more powerless than when we cannot help those we love. Yet your presence and caring, gifts of the powerless, are priceless gifts even though they may not feel like it."

Certain feelings are also natural when we are receiving care. Helplessness is again one of these. We never wanted to be a burden to someone we love. Illness calls into question our normal expectations about our bodies and their capacities. When we are free of illness we take this relationship for granted. Now we cannot count on our bodies and must give much more detailed attention to activities which were previously simple, such as negotiating a path from house to car. In the experience of illness we are reminded of our limitations, our dependencies, and our ultimate mortality. We cannot eat without nausea or move without great effort or pain; we never feel quite well. Depression often accompanies a physical illness. When depressed, we are withdrawn and self-preoccupied. This inability to transcend our self-interest is painful, and leads to self-blame. Our own needs intensify and we have little interest or ability to attend to the inner world and needs of others. We enter a place where receiving love, allowing ourselves to be loved, becomes the only path available to us.

It may seem obvious, but one of our basic needs as a person being cared for is the truth. In the absence of this we pick up nonverbal cues and sometimes misread them. We need to have our condition or illness explained to us in words we can understand, and to be consulted about its treatment. Our direct questions about our diagnosis and future deserve honest responses. We may not be able to take the truth all at once, however, and this is where it is helpful if persons respect our pace and process. They may need to walk us step-by-step through it, sensitive to the size of our shock and fear, and the enormity of our loss. Part of the care we need is support in growing spiritually during such times.

Listening to emotions brings caring into the concrete moment, away from abstract "Thou shalts" and "Thou shalt nots." We begin not by solving a problem, but by sharing a feeling. What is to be done flows from the relationship itself. We learn to ask: What can I do? What do you need? How can I help? The commitment to care is then seen as a living process that takes into account all that is happening to us in the present. This is more in keeping with the way in which women approach moral issues—not primarily as matters of principles, reasoning, and judgment, but in terms of the concrete elements of situations.[5]

This sense of the complex fabric of care is movingly portrayed in the film, *The Whales of August*. Set in a small Maine house on rocks facing out to sea, it is the story of two elderly sisters, both widows. Libby is blind and has a short temper; Sarah takes care of her as they try to get along in spite of being very different. In one scene, the two quarrel openly and it appears the caregiving relationship cannot go on. Libby declares: "Life fooled me. It always does." She has stopped living and awaits death. Sarah has more living to do; she is not done with trying new things. It is the eventual change in the bitter Libby that takes us by surprise. As the film ends, she draws on her relationship with Sarah to turn toward life once again.

Acknowledging the Limits of Care

Actual caring can be undermined by an ideal of what it should be. We then suffer from the tyranny of the impossible. It is helpful not to expect too much of ourselves. We will be strong at times; at others, we will fall apart. Some days we will be carried by optimism; at other times, we will find ourselves in the grip of fear and sadness. This coming to terms with the real applies as well to decisions about care. If a parent has been abusive, their care may need to be entrusted to others, for the safety and healing of all involved. A decision to care for someone at home may need to reconsidered if it becomes clear that this has become impossible under changed circumstances.

The dilemma of caring is that it asks us not only to hold to, take care of, empathize and suffer with those we love, but also to step back from and let go of them. We want desperately to make everything all right for those we love, and we are pained when we cannot do so. Those receiving care frequently know the limits of what we can do. They know we are not God, that we cannot cure them. What they are asking is that we do what we can; our ability to do that requires that we know as well what we cannot do.[6]

Not only are there limits to what we can do; there are limits to what we can bear. We can stand only so much contact with pain and suffering; we need renewing experiences ourselves. Time away is essential.

We cannot look unblinkingly at suffering any more than we can stare fixedly at the sun. A parent is dying. At such a time, how can we enjoy the first blossoms of spring? A loved one is in a nursing home or hospital. How can we go out to dinner with a friend? Is it OK to take time out from caring for a spouse to visit a museum? Yes. In fact, these are ways of resisting evil, ways of celebrating the goodness of life. Without such reminders of the beauty of creation, we risk losing our ability to work against suffering. We come close to despair.

It is also freeing to admit that we will fail those we care for in many ways, often in spite of our best intentions. When I was a social worker in a nursing center for several years, I developed a simple ritual for myself which acknowledged this. After the death of a resident I had cared for, I would spend a few moments in that person's room. First I recalled their presence and then I thanked them for all they had taught me, all they had given me. Finally I asked their forgiveness for the ways I had failed them—those I was aware of and those I would never know.

Receiving the Gifts of Care

Sheila Cassidy, a physician who is medical director of St. Luke's Hospice in Plymouth, England, struggles with the spiritual dimensions of caring in her book, *Sharing the Darkness*.[7] Cassidy had earlier gone to Chile to work among the very poor. One day friends asked her to treat a man with a bullet wound, a revolutionary in hiding from the secret police. For this act, she was imprisoned and tortured by the military. That experience led ultimately to her work with terminal cancer patients.

How, Cassidy wonders, is it possible to enter into another's suffering without being overwhelmed, drained, and useless? One key for her is the way she finds her humanity affirmed and redeemed by those she serves. To be with and to listen to people in pain, we must be able to hear all that is painful and dying in our own being. We come deeply to believe that the world is not divided into the sick and those who care for them. We are all both caring and cared for. If we recognize this, we will be able to come close enough to those for whom we care to enable them to call us to truth and compassion. A woman with a progressive neurological disease put it this way. She believed, she said, that a person who could see her contorted and drooling when speaking and get past their revulsion, who could get to know the person inside, would touch the core of humanity. They would then not be afraid to be in a similar situation.

Receptivity is an intrinsic element in caring. It is a readiness to receive from, as well as give to, others. Although the ideal of self-sacrificing love leads us to believe otherwise, we eventually resent giving when we experience endless criticism and no appreciation. Likewise, we find it demeaning to receive when we think we have nothing to offer in return. A good relationship is something highly valued by both the one giving and the one receiving care. It leads to a mutual sense of competence and self-esteem. When I was with my brother after his surgery, he would often ask: "And how are you doin', Kathy? Are you doin' OK?" At first I found the question somewhat startling and I was at a loss to answer. Then I came to see it, like his frequent expressions of appreciation, as part of his gracious style of dealing with a very difficult time. It was important to him that we both make it through those days as well as possible. In fact, it is in situations of care that we experience many of life's most priceless moments. Nonessentials drop away, making room for greater intimacy.

In *Caring*, her study of a female view of ethics, Nel Noddings maintains that since caring is a relationship of reciprocity, both parties must contribute to it. We are reminded of our fundamental relatedness; each of us is dependent on the other. We usually identify this dependence with the person who is ill or in need, but Noddings shows how important the person receiving care is to the quality of the relationship. An action must somehow be completed in the other if it is to be described as caring. We are, she says, dependent on one another even for our own goodness. Further, one of the most sustaining gifts of caring—the feeling of joy—comes from this fulfillment of relatedness. Joy occurs, even in the midst of grief and pain, when we find ourselves genuinely joined to another.[8] Filled by the caring relationship itself in this way, our wells of compassion are less likely to run dry.

A daughter describes one way in which those being cared for enhance the quality of care. She learns that her dad has died in a nursing home eighty-five miles away. It is December, she is battling the flu, and the roads are icy and hazardous. She makes the initial funeral arrangements as best she can over the telephone.

> I was able to take care of so many arrangements over the telephone because of the thoughtfulness of my parents. They had looked ahead to see how they might help with their future care and had given me power of attorney, made a will, bought burial plots, erected a stone, and told me what funeral home they wanted. What wonderful and caring parents.[9]

We all know ways in which the exchange does not go this well; in fact, persons being cared for can make the experience especially difficult or even intolerable. What they bring to the relationship may be endless criticism and resentment of time not devoted to their concerns; opposition to any changes or suggestions; or a long-standing spiritual emptiness that they are now asking others to fill for them. We often need much love and support from other circles of relatives and friends in order to continue giving care in such situations.

Wendy Lustbader describes the dilemmas of dependency and the importance of mutuality beautifully in *Counting on Kindness*. The expectation that we will be able to count on kindness during our times of need is, she says, a sustaining conviction. We hope that if we become incapacitated, our friends and relatives will stand by us, and that they will do so out of affection rather than pity. We also hope that we will bear our difficulties with enough grace to inspire their continued loyalty, for "we suspect that the measure of a good life is how we are treated at the end."[10]

Finding the Balance in Caring

I remember one particularly moving family interview from my years of social work in a nursing center. The woman sitting in front of me that day was pale and distraught. She had brought her husband to the nursing home because her own doctor had ordered her to do so. For over a year since the worsening of his Alzheimer's disease, she had tried to care for him at home. Times of day were twisted into hopeless confusion in his mind and he often got up at night, dressed, and stood ready to go out. The woman went to work many times with little or no sleep. She herself had a heart condition, and it was partly concern about her health that prompted her doctor's directive. As the woman told me about the preceding months, she began to sob: "The worst thing, the very worst," she said, "is that I am beginning to feel like I hate him."

It is not hard to see that caregiving requires a deep and constant caring for self. But we find ourselves in conflict as we weigh competing demands. We try to spread our limited resources among endless claims and desires, knowing that there is simply not enough to cover them all. Women bear the costs of care personally in terms of lost sleep and health, stressed relationships, compromised personal goals. When resentment starts to rise, we fear it is because we do not know how to love, that we are no longer generous enough to care for others.

Resentment is rather the signal that things are out of balance. It usually appears when our own needs are neglected for too long.

We cannot postpone the care of self until all other claims are met; it must happen all along the way. A friend who has cared lovingly and faithfully for her parents for many years says that she fears she has begun to lose heart: "There's no end to it. I realize that they could live to be a hundred. One day you take stock and see that you've given your whole life to it. Each time a new crisis comes, I think this could be the last time I do it, so I beat my brains out. But it's never the last time; it goes on and on." Another woman told me she stood in her living room one day and shouted: "When will my time come?" That so startled her husband and children that they all began to talk about what she might like and need.

Many women spend a lifetime in caregiving: raising children, supporting aging parents, being there for friends in need. They do not want to stop caring; it is a satisfying source of meaning and identity. A woman in her fifties says she bristles if someone labels the raising of her son while a single parent as self-sacrifice. She believes it was one of her life's greatest joys and satisfactions. To take it away or destroy its meaning would be to lessen her identity, who she is now and has been over the years. To feel no longer of use is one of the sorrows of age, as conveyed by the Jewish tale: "A young woman once said to an old woman, 'what is life's heaviest burden?' And the old woman said, 'to have nothing to carry.'"

It is not the caring itself that is the problem, but the dilemma of finding time and energy for all that is asked of us. This means constantly restoring the kind of balance that allows us to keep caring for ourselves as well as others. These efforts can make the caring exchange itself stronger. A daughter writes about being with her mother who was dying of cancer.

> In the next couple of weeks Mom and I had a few intimate exchanges, but one regret is that I didn't tell her of the emptiness I feared her loss would bring to me. I kept thinking "she needs to talk about her fears," not recognizing my need to talk with her. The sharing and reflecting upon our lives that I had hoped for never occurred.[11]

Not only do we lose opportunities for greater closeness when we fail to take time for ourselves, our caring itself deteriorates. The help we give has a hard, impatient edge to it that increases the sense others have that they are a burden to us. Truly, one of the best ways to care for others is to care well for ourselves.

In addition to making regular time for our own needs and interests, this self-care includes permission to enjoy the ordinary comforts and pleasures of life even when someone we love is suffering. Denying ourselves does not reduce another's suffering; it only limits our ability to bear it. In fact, it is possible that we will appreciate small things even more during these times. Madeleine L'Engle calls this a gift born of pain. As she struggles with the reality of her husband's cancer, she says:

> I am poignantly aware of the glory of the fair-weather clouds constantly moving in the blue summer sky; of the deliciousness of food, especially the fresh vegetables as we bring them in from the garden; the softness of newly washed sheets.[12]

Much caring takes place in what might be called ordinary time, in the basic experiences of human life—bathing, cooking, eating, cleaning. It is important to cherish and celebrate these moments.

Self-care also requires an accurate understanding of empathy.[13] In caring, we enter into another's feelings. This is a strength, but it is also important to distinguish our feelings from those of the other person. Our boundaries may be so permeable that we are too sensitive to the distress of others. We need to keep a separate sense of self: This is your suffering, not mine, and I do not help you by suffering it myself. Acting on our own behalf also helps with this. When we increase self-empathy, we establish a kind of boundedness that enables us to direct our sense of understanding and responsibility toward ourselves as well as others.

Widening the Circle of Support

Recently I spoke with a friend whose mother died after several months in a nursing home. My friend had resisted putting her there, and only did so after a major stroke made it impossible for the family to continue caring for her at home. To her surprise, her mother found that the staff became like a second family to her. "They loved her and she loved them," my friend said. "They cared for her so well. She was happy there."

With the lengthening of life expectancy, more of us will be relying in our later years on the kindness of strangers. Not only is our society aging with more adults reaching sixty-five, but the age structure of the elderly population is itself shifting; there are increasing proportions of very old people. We are more likely to have chronic disabilities and dependencies when we reach these very late years. This means that after prolonged and strenuous efforts to care for us, families may reach the limits of their resources and endurance. In addition, the configuration of the family is itself changing. If we believe that all the help we need should be provided by family members, and that they could give it if they were unselfish, better organized, or emotionally strong enough, we will destroy the possibility of the kind of care we need.[14] It is a mistake to view help given by those other than family as a sign that our family has failed us. Another, more useful way, is to see it as a widening of the circle of care. In Christian terms, it is an acknowledgement that we are all one body, dependent throughout our lives on the gifts of others, as they are on ours.

Caring and nurturance, traditionally considered women's work, have been discounted and treated as costly distractions from the world of business and commerce. In this way, society has neglected one of the most basic works of love.[15] Practically, this means that a woman must maintain her regular job performance while a loved one needs her to shop, cook, and take them to appointments; when a spouse or friend is recovering from surgery or struggling with a chronic disease; when a family member is in the midst of the dying process. One woman expressed it simply: "It is nearly impossible to go on with your job when someone you love deeply is that close to death. Nothing else matters as much."

What makes it possible at all is a personal network of help and support: someone at work covers for you so that you can visit a friend in the hospital, a friend checks on an aging parent when you are out of town, a neighbor answers your call when there is an emergency, friends uphold you with prayer and practical action when bad news seems too hard to bear. A participant in one of my workshops on caregiving told me that her parish had a "Love Bank." It was a way of exchanging practical help. You deposited in the bank according to your gifts and time—making visits, cooking meals, balancing checkbooks, driving people to appointments, doing household tasks—and turned to the bank for some of the same things when you yourself were in need. The image has stayed with me as a way of describing a kind of community built on the mutual giving and receiving of care.

While informal support networks will always be necessary, change must come in the way society itself allows for the importance of care.

We all rely every day on the kindness of strangers. Yet it is hard for us to think in terms of collective responsibility. In this, as in so many areas, we as women simply assume that the fault lies with ourselves, not with a situation that is historically new and not solvable on an individual basis. A combination of increased life expectancies, especially at very old ages, and women's increased participation in the labor force, has created a crisis for an expanding number of women in America.[16] We have contributed to this situation by assigning women the role of caregivers without providing them with the resources to do it— resources such as respite care, employee leave for family care, and affordable home health care.

Large numbers of people, both young and old, will require care in the future. How can we build on women's natural gifts for caring to create a different kind of society? Can we see this capacity for nurturing as belonging to men as well as women? Can we as communities and nations structure new ways of meeting human needs? A spirituality of care attuned to our changing times calls us all to create more effective forms of care for the future.

FOR PRAYER AND REFLECTION

1. Mantric Prayers

A mantra is a word or short phrase of about seven syllables. Its repetition helps us center and come to stillness. Mantric prayer can be a helpful way to pray when we are awake in the early hours of the morning and cannot sleep, when we are engaged in the tasks of caregiving, or when with someone who is dying. The following are some mantric prayers; let them lead you to create your own:

—*When praying alone:*
   You are with me every moment.
   My soul silently awaits you.
   Let me know you are present.
   Fill me with your love at dawn.
   Still my trembling mind and heart.

—*When praying with others:*
   You have put joy in our hearts.
   Gracious God, be with us now.
   Send us your love and your strength.

Show us the path to your peace.
We trust in your tender care.

2. A Lament for Physical or Mental Loss

Opening Chant or Instrumental Music

Reading: When the sixth hour came there was darkness over the whole land until the ninth hour. And at the ninth hour Jesus cried out in a loud voice, "Eloi, Eloi, lama sabachthani?" which means, "My God, my God, why have you forsaken me?" (Mk 15:33–34).

Lamentations:

All this has come upon us,
 though we have not forgotten you,
 or been false to your covenant.
Our heart has not turned back,
 nor have our steps departed from your way,
 that you should have broken us in the place
 where jackals live,
 and covered us with deep darkness (Ps 44:17–19).

Silent Meditation

Closing Prayer:

Hidden God,
You are a midwife who works with those in pain to bring
 about the new creation. May your healing support us
 in our struggle.
You are a mothering bird who shelters those in difficulty
 under the protective shadow of your wings. Hover over
 our troubled hearts.
Come to our help. Bear us up. Be with us in our confusion
 and sorrow. Deepen our sense of what remains to us amid
 our losses. Strengthen our faith that your divine
 compassion is present in ways we cannot see or understand.
 We count on your love and mercy. Amen.

Chapter 9

Legacies

A woman told me that she recently attended her aunt's funeral and then visited her deceased uncle's ranch which was up for sale. She described how she climbed over the chain around the gate, touched the earth, and watched the rattlesnakes. She noticed her uncle's personal touches on the barn and remembered the mornings of waking as a child and going outside with him as he said: "I own all the land as far as you can see." As she gazed at the land, she saw again in memory her father riding a horse, one of the few times he was free and happy. Her aunt was the last of that generation; they were all dead now. What she experienced at the funeral and while visiting the ranch, she said, was a strong sense of connection down through the generations.

A woman's spirituality is linked to all those who have come before and those who will follow after her. This interdependence of the generations becomes increasingly apparent as we age. We grow conscious of the crucial continuities between past and present, and the responsibility to insure a future for others. We are increasingly aware of the ways in which both grace and evil wash down the generations. It is time to be intentional about our legacies.

Giving and Receiving a Spiritual Legacy

When parents or older relatives and friends die, they leave an empty place against the sky. We discover that there is no one ahead of us to mark the trail, to buffer us against the dark. It is a lonely feeling. Then we gradually realize that we now play that role. At some point we inherit the legacy and become the keeper of traditions. From myth and legend, from anthropologists and historians, we learn that the elders of society are the transmitters of tradition, the guardians of ancestral values, and the providers of continuity. This contributes to the harmony of the social fabric and the interdependence of all age groups.

In 1986, when she was seventy, novelist Amy Tan's mother asked her, "If I die, what would you remember? I think you know little percent of me." A short time later, Tan's mother was taken to the hospital with what was presumed to be a heart attack. Tan promised that if her mother lived, she would take her back to China to learn about her past. She keeps this promise, and begins to discover her mother's legacy. In fact, she learns of many women's tremendous strength in the midst of adversity. Toward the close of *The Kitchen God's Wife*, watching and listening to her mother and Auntie Helen, the daughter in the novel observes:

> I watch them continue to argue, although perhaps it is not arguing. They are remembering together, dreaming together. They can already see it, the walk up the mountain, that time they were so young, when they believed their lives lay ahead of them and all good things were still possible. And the water is just as they imagined, heavy as gold, sweet as rare flower seeds.[2]

Like the fictional daughter she has created, Tan receives the wisdom passed on by these women.

Interaction across the generations both strengthens and challenges the spirituality of each individual. One thing younger members of a society have not yet learned to do is grow old and die. They rely on elders to teach them this. In turn, as we age, we find that younger friends and relatives affect our lives in many ways. In our era, those dying of AIDS and violence have become a whole generation of the young who are now teaching older generations about dying and grief. We create in one another qualities such as courage, hope, or despair. While older persons who are closed and bitter trigger in us a dread of our own aging, women who find their later years a positive adventure, who discover new sources of creativity and freedom as they age, and who share the wisdom accumulated over a lifetime, give everyone hope. Our ancestors have shaped us in numerous ways by the quality of their presence to us and the world. We do the same for our successors. We now have families of four or five generations. This creates complex patterns and legacies. The paths of influence are intricate and move in all directions.

A woman recently shared a vivid example of how our spirituality emerges from an intergenerational matrix. The decline of her father, in his late eighties, surfaced her grief at the thought of losing someone so important to her. In addition, as they tried to settle a number of medical decisions, she became aware that talking to her father made her own death, and her struggle with fears of it, more real. While she was working through these issues, she received a letter from an adult son, asking her to enter into a process of reconciling some old conflicts. This woman's calls to conversion sprang from both sides of the web of human life.

This circle of spiritual sharing was strengthened in another way by a woman who taught her daughter the Jesus Prayer when she was in the hospital and afraid. The daughter, in turn, taught the prayer to her daughter.

Although it is important to deal with questions surrounding the material legacies we will bequeath to others, it is the spiritual inheritance which is most significant. Several women have described to me the gifts they received from watching women in their family deal with aging. One told me that her mother was always in charge and ran everything in their home. Now, in her later years, she has become much more vulnerable, and my friend says that vulnerability has enabled her to relate to her mother in a whole new way. Another told how her mother, through her way of dying, taught her family how to live. During her final days, her mother was unable to speak because of a respirator tube, but she did not stop communicating with her family. She used a felt tip pen and a white enamel clipboard to write instructions about her funeral arrangements and to continue to teach them about life and death in mantra-like statements: "Life is honest and serious." "Dying is for the birds!" "See you in heaven, wherever that is." She blew her family kisses each time they left her bedside.[3]

But our spiritual inheritance can be burden as well as gift. We may find that what we are blown from the bedside of an older friend or relative is far from kisses. Unrelieved negativity, resistance to all attempts at kindness, refusal to acknowledge and deal with the facts of aging—these become the realities with which those close to a person must struggle. They poison the ancestral well from which all members drink. Once a young girl stopped me as she was leaving our nursing center with her mother, and asked: "How much love do you think it will take before my grandma can be happy?" It is not struggles shared, sadness acknowledged, or the imperfect ways in which we all come to terms with difficulty that constitute this negative inheritance. It is, rather, in the biblical image, the heart of stone that refuses to become a heart of flesh.

In the exchange between the generations, time itself can take on a new quality. Earlier moments of our lives overlap with the present, and we discover common experiences that transcend age differences. One afternoon several years ago my mother tripped and fell down the stairs at home, landing on her head on the concrete basement floor. She suffered a severe head and brain injury but, incredible survivor that she is, managed gradually to recover. During the first weeks of her return from the hospital, she needed someone with her at all times, so I took off work and went home to care for her. Part of our routine each day was to walk back and forth on the sun porch while I provided the physical support she needed to maintain her balance and regain her confidence that she could walk. On one of these afternoons she turned and said to me: "It's a funny thing. I taught you how to walk, and here you are now helping me to learn it all over again." It was not that I was now parent and my mother, child. This would have been a denial of the far more complex truth of the moment. She was still teaching me how to walk. We all keep returning to places that are familiar yet not the same. Two moments of time fuse. Periods of the life cycle weave in and out of one another and connect in ways difficult to convey. A friend shared a similar story regarding her own mother who was frightened by a heart condition, exhausted by doctors' appointments, and unable to sleep. She crawled into bed with her and held her, saying: "You're just stressed out by all of this." Her mother fell asleep in her arms.

Trees of Life

One of the things all generations crave is knowledge of their past. We need long-lived narratives, stories of human relationships with historical depth. Myths, folk tales, proverbs, stories, and songs—these tell us who we are and who we can be. That is why storytelling is such a vital gift to succeeding generations. We want to know about the land and people that first nurtured us. Where did our ancestors come from? What were the smells, the seasons, the landscapes that shaped them and, ultimately, us?

In an age of genetic research we need information on family diseases and deaths to instruct us about our own health and vulnerabilities. Family trees tell us about marriages and children, divorces and cutoffs. We begin to recognize inherited patterns and propensities. A daughter told me that once when her mother was reminiscing, she related how, when a young girl, she had been the one to find her aunt dead, and had run crying into the street. This gave the daughter insight into some of her own anxieties that she had never understood.

Stories are not only about families; they are about cultural inheritances. For theologian Katie Geneva Cannon, the creative storytelling of her mother was what linked her to the origin of black people in America. In *Inheriting Our Mothers' Gardens*, she tells how her mother is able to pass on eyewitness accounts from freed relatives to succeeding generations: stories of a father who was the only free child in his family; stories of a grandmother who, when freedom finally came, walked hundreds of miles from plantation to plantation looking for the children taken from her and sold as slaves. Her mother always includes music in her storytelling. This black sacred music is a vital part of her family's religious tradition, spirituals that express faith, sorrow, celebration, and protest.

> O Freedom! O Freedom!
> O Freedom, I love thee!
> And before I be a slave,
> I'll be buried in my grave,
> And go home to my Lord and be free.

Tales, songs, and prayers are part of Cannon's inheritance, the cultural windows through which she learns her people's response to the dehumanizing presence of slavery and plantation life. As direct descendants of African-American slaves, Cannon says her family draws from such traditions confidence and spiritual endurance in the midst of oppression.[4]

Stories tell us what we need to know not only about ourselves and our culture, but about our civilization. Long memory conveys what we cannot see in the immediate situation. Sister Mary Evangeline, SNJM, shows what this means for understanding war and peace. In her thoughts on her ninetieth birthday in 1981, she writes:

> Five times within my life I've seen our boys (that means
> brothers, friends, and neighbors)

March off with beating drums and gallant hopes "to make
    the world safe for Democracy" or
    "to save our Country's honor" or
    "the freedom of the world" as fought in foreign
    lands.
But when bedraggled legions returned in disillusion—
Some with dangling, empty sleeves where muscled arms
    had been,
And others dragging crutches; some with vacant stares of
    gassed and shell-shocked victims;
Some did not return—and weeping mothers hung gold
    stars in windows
As symbol of their sacrifice—and as I viewed the
    ravages of war
I knew that war was not the answer to the problems of
    the world.[5]

Stories convey truths honed through hours and years of meditation.

As part of a tree of life, we also count on being remembered. The ancient Hebrews believed that the ultimate hell was being forgotten, erased from memory. Often small mementos—a jewelry case, a lace handkerchief, a snapshot—enable others to hold us in mind, to keep us in memory. The same is true of those mementos we receive. They strengthen the links between us and those who have gone before. Their loss creates a kind of extinction. Sometimes it is a person's voice that goes with us. One woman said that an older friend who died the previous year was the person who had always reminded her of the importance of taking care of herself: "How will I know when I am not doing this? When I hear Martha's voice talking to me. It's mostly when I'm looking in the mirror. I hear her saying, 'Look at all those dark circles under your eyes.'"

Celebrations are another way of remembering others. The ceremonial ties that hold generations together over time may be as simple as a holiday recipe or a date for a reunion. In *Having Our Say: The Delany Sisters' First 100 Years*, Sarah and Elizabeth Delany talk about people who have died so long ago that they are the only ones who still have any memory of them. They say they always find ways to celebrate these memories of family and friends: "Why, we still have a birthday party for Papa, even though he's been gone since 1928. We cook his favorite birthday meal, just the way he liked it." The menu for this party includes chicken and gravy, rice and sweet potatoes, ham, macaroni and cheese, cabbage, cauliflower, broccoli, turnips, carrots, and a birthday cake—pound cake and ambrosia made from oranges and fresh coconut.[6] A feast of memories.

Grandparenting and Grace

A woman recently told me: "The greatest single grace of the past year was becoming a grandparent." Another said that being a part of the birth of her grandchild was one of the most important religious experiences of her life. Afterward she took the hands of her two other grandchildren and walked to the cathedral. Somehow after the birth, she wanted to take them in to worship, to tell them something about the religious traditions that went back so many centuries. Dismayed to find the cathedral locked, they knelt on the steps outside and said a prayer.

Grandparenting is clearly a locus of grace that moves in both directions. Grandchildren call forth new realities in their grandparents: a sense of wonder and play, laughter and adventure. In showing children the world, we taste, touch, smell, and see it again as if for the first time. If we want them to smell a rose, name a daffodil, or eat a strawberry, we must enter the experience with them.

The love of a grandparent is often one of the strongest experiences a child has of unconditional love. When teaching courses on ministry with the aging, I sometimes ask students to begin with an exercise in which they relive a memory of an older person who was especially significant to them, bringing back the emotional power of that person's presence. I have been struck by how often students remember a grandparent who loved them in a way that helped them believe in themselves and their gifts. This healing power of a grandmother's love is communicated beautifully by a Puerto Rican woman named Inez. She speaks of how God is a dark mystery to her:

> But if they would ask me to draw God, I would draw my grandmother smiling. Because she is the only person that I believe has filled me or filled me so much that I can compare her with God. I would draw a picture of my grandmother with her hands open, smiling, as if to say, "Come with me because I am waiting for you." God is strength for the *lucha* (struggle), strength to keep going, to encourage.[7]

This is grandmother as image of divine love and acceptance, as source of courage for life.

The grandmother in the powerful Chicano novel *Bless Me, Ultima*, is above all else, a healer.

> "And the children?" my father asked. I knew why he expressed concern for me and my sisters. It was because Ultima was *curandera*, a woman who knew herbs and remedies of the ancients, a miracle-worker who could heal the sick. And I had heard that Ultima could lift the curses laid by *brujas* (witches), and that she could exorcise the evil the witches planted in people to make them sick. And because a *curandera* had this power she was misunderstood and often suspected of practicing witchcraft herself.[8]

In her role of healer, the older Hispanic woman shepherds her family, nourishes their spirits. She also fulfills the role of *pasionaria* or *pastora* to her people by passing on an oral tradition that captures their experience and reflects their faith histories. The grandmothers, or *abuelitas*, are the central figures in the transmitting of the wisdom found in these stories and prayers. And though mothers and fathers are expected to give blessings, it is the grandmother's blessing that is most prized in the Hispanic family.[9]

There are no blueprints for being a grandparent today. Babies affected by the drug culture are now at times being parented primarily by their grandparents. There is less geographical stability, and the extended family is often broken up as people move around the country. Divorce creates complications and sometimes means a struggle to remain in contact with grandchildren. Family itself is being defined in new ways. But in and through all the reconfigurations, grandparenting remains a very significant relationship between the generations. In a 1983 conference exploring the theme, grandparents were seen as symbols of connectedness within and across lives; as people who can listen and have the time to do so; as persons with time to give help, and attention; as links to known and unknown pasts; and as people who are sufficiently varied, flexible, and complex to defy easy categories and clear-cut roles. The most important spiritual role that grandparents play is simply *being there*. It is their presence, more than any specific action, that makes a difference.[10]

It is not necessary to have biological grandchildren in order to be a part of this intergenerational weaving. We can share in it in many ways. The movement toward multigenerational living is one.

There are thousands of wonderful old people, living alone in thousands of houses all over America. More often than not, they are lonely, isolated and frightened. There are also thousands of younger people who would like to live with them, not as boarders, but as friends. I emphasize the word "friends," because that is what multigenerational living is, at its best.[11]

Often groups of older and younger people living together become intentional families, sharing care and nurturance as well as the tasks of maintaining a household.

In the nursing center where I worked, there was a woman who had survived two strokes. Weak and with greatly diminished abilities to care for herself, she tried to figure out why she was still alive. What came to her was that she was here as the sole member of her generation to witness to and rejoice in the gifts of her brothers' children. Her brothers had not lived to see this generation, and she had. Another woman, seven years into her own retirement, became concerned about children who come home to an empty house because their parents must work. Recognizing what a need was there, she conceived the idea of Dial-A-Gram, providing a friendly voice to ease the loneliness or fear of such children. She developed a list of references and a flier describing her free service, met with principals of local schools, and got information from parents and children. Her goal was to make a difference to a generation of children she feared were at risk.

Women as Mentors

One key role we as older women play for persons of all ages is that of mentor. This ministry flows both from who we are and what we do. A friend in her late forties who works in a health clinic told me the following story. A woman of eighty-three came for a check-up. She said that for the past two years she had been slowly going blind and her sight was now nearly gone in both eyes. However, if she held a magnifying glass in front of one eye, she could see a little at a time. "The worst thing is," she said, "I can't paint." She added that after her husband's death twenty years earlier, she had begun to fulfill a lifelong dream of being a painter. At first she had read books about painting, but she couldn't learn fast enough, so she started taking classes. Soon she was finishing her work around the house by ten in the morning and painting until four, forgetting completely about the time or the need to eat. In the evening she would return to the painting, and before she knew it, it would be three in the morning. She hadn't intended to sell her work, but a friend who was visiting one day offered her money for one of her paintings. Soon she was able to sell enough to buy paints and canvases. "You see," she said, "I always knew from the time I was a child that I was meant to be a painter. As a little girl, I used to sit outside and sketch the barn."

My friend listened in astonished silence as this woman poured out her story, then she said: "I can't believe you are telling me this. I feel as if you were sent to me. I, too, have known since childhood that I was meant to paint. I have just now found the courage to sign up for a class. Your message to me is: 'Don't let your dream die. Paint.' Later, as the woman was preparing to leave the clinic, she asked to see the younger woman again. She gave her a phone number and address and said: "I have twelve paintings left. Would you like to see them?" "I will come," my friend replied. She knew she had found a mentor.

Mentors are those who have walked before us on the path we want to take. They are trusted guides. As companions on our way they use their familiarity with the landscape to reassure us when we become afraid and lose heart, and to let us know that others traveling this way have also been through what we are experiencing. With a wider, longer lens they are able to see potential in us that we may not be able to glimpse ourselves. What can be said of them is like the tribute given to Dorothy Day:

> I am grateful beyond words for the grace of this woman's life, for her sensible, unflinching rightness of mind, her long and lonely truth, her journey to the heart of things. I think of her as one who simply helped us, in a time of self-inflicted blindness, to see.[12]

Each of us can name persons who have been this for us and to whom we are immensely grateful.

The role of mentor can be quite informal, merged with that of friend. Or it can be more formally established in a parish or community. Life experiences prepare older women to be spiritual mentors and grief counselors. Women who have spent a lifetime in caregiving sometimes shrink from the thought of yet another relationship where they are the one nurturing. However, mentoring does not mean setting aside our own goals in order to sponsor or support another. The most powerful mentoring comes from those who are continuing to use and develop their own gifts. A woman was drawn to a scripture course offered by an eighty-year-old woman in her parish. "Here was a woman who was older and still growing," she said. "I wanted to find out how she was doing it."

A resident who lived at a shelter for homeless women reflected on the experience as she was about to leave. She believed being homeless was more than not having a roof over your head. She saw it rather as about being bewildered, about losing one's identity, familiar surroundings, and confidence that you can find a way out. During her time at the shelter, mentoring was for her often a spontaneous thing.

> It's sort of a surrealistic potluck, with everyone bringing her own past, and taking from the past of others, the wisdom and compassion offered.[13]

A mentor, she believed, is someone who tells the truth about her life.

Finishing Well

Talk of spiritual legacies can be discouraging. Perhaps others are cut out to be role models for succeeding generations, but we ourselves feel quite ordinary, barely able to cope with our own problems. The same is true of the notion of finishing well. It conveys a kind of completion and perfection that eludes most of us. More often, we need to know that what we are doing is good enough, even when it feels so small.

And yet, the longer life span now open to us offers opportunities never before available for exchange, healing, and intimacy between the generations. If we make use of them, we have decades, rather than days, to resolve unfinished business, to become separate enough to establish new ways of relating. As I listen to members of all generations work toward this kind of closeness, the following ideas strike me as especially important.

1. *Trying to create understanding between the generations is itself an act of love, even if the fruits are long in coming.* We are geared to outcomes. We wait for it to be all made right. But conversations between generations are an ongoing dialogue. There will be conflict. There may be breaks in the conversation, setbacks, explosive moments. The fact that we are on the way is more important than that we have arrived. In fact, we may not arrive, or the goal may change by the time we get there. It is not possible to set things right once and for all.

Rather, renewal is a continual work entrusted to every generation. We recognize it not in final, perfected states, but in small moments of redemption.

This focus on process is a natural part of women's approach to life, but it frames the situation well. Relationships between the generations need room to change and deepen over time. That between adult children and their parents illustrates this. What adult children often want is the ability to express their current experiences and perceptions without being judged or advised. They wish for recognition and integrity. They want to know their parents as adult persons, not as mothers or fathers. This means understanding their parents' feelings and experiences, knowing more about their lives. They desire more adult mutuality. A daughter found this with her father in a painful moment: "I told my dad, 'I worry about your driving, that you will hurt yourself or someone else.' He told me, 'My world is shrinking terribly.' I cried and he cried."

2. *It is important to give the gifts we want to give, and address the issues that stand between us,* now. In this way we avoid endlessly postponing expressions of love, forgiveness, and regret: Someday I will ask about these things I have always wanted to know. Someday I will tell this person how much she means to me. Someday I will broach the difficult topics.

In her interviews with rural elderly, a physician is told by Annie Lane, who is seventy-one at the time of the conversation:

> I tell people, "Don't send me flowers when I'm dead. I want them now." It wouldn't do me two cents worth of good after I'm dead to put me in my grave and put a pile of flowers on me as big as this house. If you've got a flower you want me to have, give it to me while I'm living.[14]

I have been a witness to many moving exchanges during the dying process. If there is spiritual and social support and effective pain control, it can be a very important transition time. Finally, there is a chance to say things one has longed to say or hear. Such conversations are privileged moments, and a great gift at any time. Postponing these until the end of life is also a long time to wait, and prevents much richness that might have been possible had it happened earlier. Once I spent several days bringing together two sisters who had been estranged for twenty-two years. One was in our nursing center, dying of cancer. Her younger sister, now very frail, lived in another part of the city. On the day of the visit, I stood outside the door after arranging their wheelchairs next to each other. I thought the sister I knew would say all that she had told me she wanted to tell her sister. Instead, they simply embraced one another and wept.

3. *Long-lasting relationships are usually very complex.* As we age, we let go of idealized pictures of our families and relationships, and begin to take in their complicated reality. With time, we learn to hold together many layers of truth. Gifts and strengths are mixed with pain and liabilities. Love intermingles with anger; a yearning for closeness, with a desire for distance. We find it difficult to hold all these conflicting emotions together within us at once. How can this person who has caused us so much pain evoke such depths of compassion and pity? Part of us wants to scream, while another part wants to weep. A woman says:

> I love my father and I feel such anger toward him. I curse him and I forgive him. I struggle daily to understand what makes him who is, and I hold him responsible for all the suffering he has caused me.

This mixture of emotions is especially poignant as friends and relatives become frail. We may feel a strange amalgam of guilt and sorrow, fear and regret, when in their presence. It is helpful to remember that such mixtures of emotion characterize most relationships that endure over many years.

4. *If something new is to happen in a relationship, each person must do his or her own spiritual work.* Before we can make peace with one another, we must begin the process of making peace with ourselves. If we each respond to our own individual promptings toward recognition of pain and anger, disclosure and open listening, acceptance and forgiveness, change can happen between us. Such spiritual growth requires support and time.

The paradox is that we are separate, and yet interdependent. On the part of a daughter, this may mean accepting her parents as human beings, and relinquishing expectations that they provide all the love she needs and wants.

> It is really hard to face the fact that it wasn't all right. That my parents had flaws and they're in me. It makes me really sad. I feel sorry for them, and for me, too.

On the part of a parent it may include acknowledgement of failures and release from impossible standards of perfection.

> You try so hard and you can't keep them from pain. They were hurt very, very much by it in spite of all your best efforts. You try to protect them. It's very hard.

Since mothers often get more blame in our culture, they need to develop kindness toward themselves, and let go of responsibility for what is the human condition. It is also helpful to situate one's mothering in historical context, to acknowledge who you were and what was available to you at the time. Often what we regret is not something that was intentional, but the result of generational tragedy—mental illness, alcoholism, abuse—touching our own lives. We help to heal this tragedy when we are able to mourn it, make peace with ourselves, and put an end to it in our interactions with the next generation.[15]

When we attend to our own growth issues, it becomes clear how we are connected to, yet separate from, a parent, friend, or child. Then their pain is not unbearable and we do not shape our identity according to their praise or criticism. We do not feel responsible for making them happy, or seeing that everything in their lives turns out all right. It is, paradoxically, this effort to become clear about ourselves that makes relationship possible. We do not ask that others—parents, children, friends—make us feel that our life is worth living.

5. *We need to make room for new possibilities in a relationship.* "I wish my daughter and I could list all the accusations we have against each other and burn them," a mother told me. "Then we could start where we are and create something new." Sometimes it is not the collecting, but the clearing out of a legacy that needs to take place.

What if the person with whom we have unfinished business dies without our having a chance to complete it? Often women want to heal the way they hold the memory of a deceased parent, relative, or friend. Steps toward bringing this about are prayer for healing, dialogue with the person, journaling, and ritual. In these ways we create a space to tell the person what we never had a chance to say, and to listen to what they would say to us now; an opportunity to release the emotions we are carrying, and to let go of what we need to relinquish. Through this process we gradually change the way this relationship lives in us.

A Planetary Inheritance

In the phases of the moon and the recurrence of the seasons we sense the deep connections that exist not only in space, but across time. The artist Meinrad Craighead says that when the sun rises over the Sandia Mountains, she starts a fire facing it in a terra cotta vessel that sits on an altar. Then her morning prayer begins. She built the altar in the center of her land near the Rio Grande, as an act of thanksgiving for her fiftieth birthday. Her prayer moves around the fire, around the four sides of the altar, honoring the cross of the four directions, the seasons, and the elements. This, she says, is our universal landscape. By the time she has made the sacred prayer circle, the fire has burned to embers, and she has spoken with the living and the dead, with ancestors, godparents, animals and the elements.[16]

Seeing all creation in relationship within our planetary circle alerts us to the scope of our legacies. We glimpse those dimly imagined descendants of ours. As civilization's elders, we cannot afford to be narrowly consumed with our own comfort and survival. Our most important legacy is to ensure that our fragile planet will have a future, that all the world's children and grandchildren who come after us will have an earth to call home.

In her book, *Models of God*, theologian Sallie McFague suggests a meditation that deepens our appreciation for this inheritance. She asks us to call up concrete images of specific events, people, plants and animals, objects and places that are precious to us. Then we are to dwell upon the uniqueness and value of these particular cherished aspects of our world, to meditate on them until the pain of contemplating their loss, not just to you or to me, but to all of life for all time, becomes unbearable.[17]

When leading a group in this form of meditation, I have sometimes asked them to mention out loud the object of their contemplation in the silence that follows the prayer. Cherished aspects of existence are countless and wide-ranging: wind and sun glancing off an intricate spider web, the opening notes of a Beethoven symphony, the smile on the face of a new grandson, the first cherry blossoms on a spring day, a full moon against a blackening sky, the sound of laughter, the welcoming face of a lifelong friend, the quiet surface of a favorite lake in the mountains, the aroma of home-made bread as it comes from the oven.

Women are keepers of tradition. A primary question for those who grew old in previous eras was the financial security, health, and happiness of the next generation. Now the question is much more stark: Will we leave our descendants an Earth on which to dwell? In one sense, all that we have explored in this book relates to this question, the heritage of love we will leave the universe. It is a crucial part of the calling and immense challenge which come to us with the gift of additional years.

FOR PRAYER AND REFLECTION

1. A Ritual for Passing On a Legacy (The legacy might be an object like a ring, a scrapbook of photos, an autobiography, or a statement of a spiritual legacy.)

Opening Song

Prayer: O God, you are the river of energy that joins all generations. Be with us as we honor the life that moves through time. Deepen in us a sense of our connection with all beings. We bless the stream that flows through us from our mother's life, our grandmother's life, the life of her mother's mother, the legacy of generations.

Blessing of the Gift (The one giving the legacy sprinkles it with water, saying:) I ask God to bless this gift of memory. May it remind us that what passes from generation to generation is a sacred trust.

Giving of the Legacy: Time is passing. Generations pass. Receive this symbol of the enduring gift of life I wish to entrust to you and those who follow you. I ask you to join me in being the keeper of traditions, the curator of our family's past and future memories.

Accepting of the Legacy: I accept this gift with joy and gratitude. May it be for me a symbol of your love, and of all that you have meant to me. May it remind me always of the blessing and promise which come from the past. The ties that hold generations together over time are precious and fragile. With you I will nurture them.

Giving of a Symbol of Gratitude (a flower, a card of thanks): Receive this symbol of my gratitude for your life and the gifts it has brought me. May it be a reminder that you are cherished and valued, and that your life has meaning beyond your own span of years.

Closing Prayer:

Your steadfast love, O God, lasts forever. You pour out your goodness on your children and their children's children, on all generations who remember, who revere you and keep covenant with you. May all creation praise you! (Based on Ps 103:17–18).

Refreshments and Celebration

2. A Ritual of Intergenerational Healing

(This ritual is meant to mark the conclusion of a conversation or process in which reconciliation has taken place. For each person there is paper, pen, a package of flower seeds, a small pot and soil for planting. A container that is safe for burning paper to ashes is provided as well.)

Opening Prayer: O God, you who desire our healing and peace, be with us as we seek to forgive one another and be reconciled. Soften the hard places in our hearts. Strengthen our resolve to let go of hurt and anger. Open us to the energy of your love and generosity. We count on your grace and power. Amen.

Reading: Jesus said, "Imagine a sower going out to sow. As the sower sowed, some seeds fell on the edge of the path, and the birds came and ate them up. Others fell on patches of rock where they found little soil and sprang up straight away, because there was no depth of earth; but as soon as the sun came up they were scorched and, not having any roots, they withered away. Others fell among thorns, and the thorns grew up and choked them. Others fell on rich soil and produced their crop, some a hundredfold, some sixty, some thirty. Listen, anyone who has ears" (Mt 13:4–9).

Quiet Music and Reflection: During this time each person writes out the things she desires to let go of in the relationship, e.g., past hurts, regrets, disappointments, anger.

Rite of Forgiveness and Letting Go: Each person tears the paper with the things she is letting go of into pieces, puts them into the container, and watches as they burn to ashes.

In turn each person then asks for and receives forgiveness for some way in which she is aware of hurting the other, e.g., First person: "I have hurt you by my accusations and lack of trust. I ask your forgiveness." Second person: "I forgive you as God has forgiven us both."

Rite of Strengthening of Bonds: Each person offers the other a package of flower seeds as a symbol of the fresh beginning they hope to find in the relationship. Each mixes part of the ashes with the soil and plants her seeds in it.

Closing Prayer (Based on Hildegard of Bingen):[18]
O Holy Spirit, Fiery Comforter Spirit,
Life of the life of all creatures,
Holy are You, You that give existence to all form.
Holy are You, You that are balm for the mortally wounded.
Holy are You, You that cleanse deep hurt.
Fire of love, breath of all holiness, You are so delicious to our hearts!
Bulwark of life, You are the hope of oneness for that which is separate.
Amen.

Music, Refreshments and Celebration

Notes

1. Visions of Ourselves

[1](New York: Penguin Books, 1979), p. 5.

[2](New York: Penguin Books, 1987), p. 149.

[3]Miriam Therese Winter, *WomanWord: A Feminist Lectionary and Psalter. Women of the New Testament* (New York: The Crossroad Publishing Company, 1991), p. 77.

[4]"Coeleen Kiebert," in Cathleen Rountree, *On Women Turning 50: Celebrating Mid-Life Discoveries* (San Francisco: HarperCollins, 1993), pp. 152–153. Another woman's global search for strong images of older women is recounted in Allegra Taylor, *Older Than Time: A Grandmother's Search for Wisdom* (London: HarperCollins, 1993).

[5](Nashville: Abingdon Press, 1983), p. 70.

[6]Polly Francis, "The Autumn of My Life," in *Songs of Experience: An Anthology of Literature on Growing Old*, ed. Margaret Fowler and Priscilla McCutcheon (New York: Ballantine Books, 1991), p. 31.

[7]"Late Mid-Life Astonishment: Disruptions to Identity and Self-Esteem," in *Faces of Women and Aging*, ed. Nancy D. Davis, Ellen Cole, and Esther D. Rothblum (New York: The Haworth Press, 1993), pp. 1–12.

[8](New York: Random House, 1983), p. 180.

[9]Elisabeth Schüssler Fiorenza, *In Memory of Her: A Feminist Theological Reconstruction of Christian Origins* (New York: The Crossroad Publishing Company, 1983), p. 130.

[10]See Elliott A. Norse, *Ancient Forests of the Pacific Northwest* (Washington, D.C.: Island Press, 1990), p. 41.

[11]Patricia Garfield, "Menopausal Dreams (An Excerpt)," in *Women of the 14th Moon: Writings on Menopause*, ed. Dena Taylor and Amber Coverdale Sumrall (Freedom, CA: The Crossing Press, 1991), p. 324.

[12]Mary Francis Shura Craig, "A Mosaic of Minutes," in *The Courage to Grow Old*, ed. Phillip L. Berman (New York: Ballantine Books, 1989), p. 6.

[13]"On A Mission," *The Seattle Times*, January 17, 1994.

[14]Martha Holstein made this point when she was associate director of the

American Society on Aging. For similar insights, see the essays in *What Does It Mean To Grow Old? Reflections from the Humanities,* ed. Thomas R. Cole and Sally A. Gadow (Durham, NC: Duke University Press, 1986).

[15](New York: Simon & Schuster, 1993).

[16]"Reflections on Elderhood: Interviews," in Eugene C. Bianchi, *Aging as a Spiritual Journey* (New York: The Crossroad Publishing Company, 1982), p. 242.

[17]Bernice L. Neugarten, ed., *Middle Age and Aging* (Chicago: University of Chicago Press, 1968), p. 94.

[18]See Kathleen Perkins, "Psychosocial Implications of Women and Retirement," *Social Work* 37 (1992), 526–532; *Women As Elders: Images, Visions, and Issues,* ed. Marilyn J. Bell (New York: The Haworth Press, 1986); and *Women on the Front Lines: Meeting the Challenge of An Aging America,* ed. Jessie Allen and Alan Pifer (Washington, D.C.: The Urban Institute Press, 1993).

[19]See Cynthia M. Taeuber and Jessie Allen, "Women in Our Aging Society: The Demographic Outlook"; and Julianne Malveaux, "Race, Poverty, and Women's Aging," in *Women on the Front Lines,* pp. 11–46 and 167–190.

[20]"Plight of Older Black Women," *The Seattle Times,* October 26, 1993. Emily Herring Wilson and Susan Mullaly convey the gifts and strength of older black women in *Hope and Dignity: Older Black Women of the South* (Philadelphia: Temple University Press, 1983).

[21]Her story is told by Patricia Mathes Cane, "A Different Perspective," in *Women of the 14th Moon,* pp. 353–354.

[22]Similar critiques have been made by others. See, for example, Eugene Bianchi, *Aging as a Spiritual Journey,* p. 29; and Stephanie Demetrakopoulos, *Listening to Our Bodies: The Rebirth of Feminine Wisdom* (Boston: Beacon Press, 1993), p. 168.

[23]See Judith V. Jordan, Alexandra G. Kaplan, Jean Baker Miller, Irene P. Stiver, and Janet L. Surrey, *Women's Growth in Connection: Writings from the Stone Center* (New York: The Guilford Press, 1991), pp. 1–3.

[24]The problems this model presents for a theology of person are very helpfully analyzed by Constance Buchanan, "The Fall of Icarus: Gender, Religion, and the Aging Society," in *Shaping New Vision: Gender and Values in American Culture,* ed. Clarissa W. Atkinson, Constance H. Buchanan, and Margaret R. Miles (Ann Arbor, Michigan: UMI Research Press, 1987), pp. 169–190.

[25]See, for example, *Women Growing Older: Psychological Perspectives,* ed. Barbara F. Turner and Lillian E. Troll (Thousand Oaks, CA: SAGE Publications, 1994).

[26]See *Women's Growth in Connection: Writings from the Stone Center.*

[27]Irene P. Stiver, "The Meanings of 'Dependency' in Female-Male

Relationships," in *Women's Growth in Connection*, p. 153. A helpful framework for understanding attachment and autonomy in psychospiritual maturity is found in Joann Wolski Conn, *Spirituality and Personal Maturity* (Mahwah, NJ: Paulist Press, 1989); and Robert Kegan, *The Evolving Self: Problem and Process in Human Development* (Cambridge, MA: Harvard University Press, 1982).

[28]See, for example, Fritjof Capra, *The Tao of Physics: An Exploration of the Parallels between Modern Physics and Eastern Mysticism* (New York: Bantam Books, 1984).

[29]For a discussion of this passage, see Gail R. O'Day, "John," in *The Women's Bible Commentary*, ed. Carol A. Newsom and Sharon H. Ringe (Louisville, Kentucky: Westminster/John Knox Press, 1992), p. 303.

[30]Wendy Lustbader, *Counting on Kindness: The Dilemmas of Dependency* (New York: The Free Press, 1991), pp. 146–147. See also Carol Gilligan, "Mapping the Moral Domain: New Images of Self in Relationship," *Cross Currents* 39 (Spring 1989), 50–63.

[31]"Teaching Creative Writing to Older Women," *Women's Studies Quarterly* 1 & 2 (1989), 54–55. The strengths of aging are also conveyed in M.F.K. Fisher, *Sister Age* (New York: Alfred A. Knopf, 1983).

[32]See Gisela Labouvie-Vief, "Women's Creativity and Images of Gender," in *Women Growing Older*, pp. 140–168.

[33]Barbara Myerhoff, *Number Our Days* (New York: Simon and Schuster, 1978), p. 241.

[34]*Number Our Days*, p. 248.

[35]See David Gutmann, *Reclaimed Powers: Toward a New Psychology of Men and Women in Later Life* (New York: Basic Books, 1987); and Margaret Hellie Huyck, "The Relevance of Psychodynamic Theories for Understanding Gender among Older Women," in *Women Growing Older*, pp. 202–238.

[36]Second Edition (Chicago: University of Illinois Press, 1992).

[37]See Helena Znaniecka Lopata, "The Widowed Family Member," in *Transitions of Aging*, ed. Nancy Datan and Nancy Lohmann (New York: Academic Press, 1980), p. 114.

[38](New York: W.W. Norton & Company, 1979), p. 15.

[39]See *Unspoken Worlds: Women's Religious Lives*, ed. Nancy Auer Falk and Rita M. Gross (Belmont, CA: Wadsworth Publishing Company, 1989); and Barbara G. Walker, *The Crone: Woman of Age, Wisdom, and Power* (San Francisco: Harper & Row, 1985).

[40]"Ellen Burstyn," in *On Women Turning 50: Celebrating Mid-Life Discoveries*, p. 18.

[41]For reflections on the role of Anna as well as a detailed discussion of widows in the New Testament and the early church, see Bonnie Bowman

Thurston, *The Widows: A Woman's Ministry in the Early Church* (Minneapolis: Fortress Press, 1989).

[42]Paula Gunn Allen, *Grandmothers of the Light: A Medicine Woman's Sourcebook* (Boston: Beacon Press, 1991, 1986), p. 15.

[43]Paula Gunn Allen, *The Sacred Hoop: Recovering the Feminine in American Indian Traditions* (Boston: Beacon Press, 1986), p. 56.

[44]See Hildegard of Bingen, *Scivias*, trans. Mother Columba Hart and Jane Bishop (Mahwah, NJ: Paulist Press, 1990), pp. 163–164 and 438; and Gabriele Uhlein, *Meditations with Hildegard of Bingen* (Santa Fe, NM: Bear & Company, 1982).

[45]Denise Levertov, "October Moonrise," in *Evening Train* (New York: New Directions Publishing Corporation, 1993), p. 12.

[46]Naomi Janowitz and Maggie Wenig, "Sabbath Prayers for Women," in *Womanspirit Rising: A Feminist Reader in Religion* (San Francisco: Harper & Row, 1979), p. 176.

2. Grace in Transitions

[1](New York: Harper & Row, 1973), p. 150.

[2]For helpful descriptions of women's transitions as we age see Mary Catherine Bateson, *Composing a Life* (New York: Penguin Books, 1989); Diana Cort-Van Arsdale and Phyllis Newman, *Transitions: A Woman's Guide to Successful Retirement* (New York: HarperCollins Publishers, 1991); Jane Porcino, *Growing Older, Getting Better: A Handbook for Women in the Second Half of Life* (Reading, MA: Addison-Wesley Publishing Company, 1993); and *Women and the Life Cycle: Transitions and Turning Points*, ed. Patricia Abbott et al. (London: Macmillan Press, 1987).

[3]In *Dance of the Spirit: The Seven Steps of Women's Spirituality* (New York: Bantam Books, 1989), Maria Harris shows how such rhythmic, repetitive circles form the pattern of women's spirituality.

[4]Sr. Mary Sarah Fasenmyer, "Ministry to the Aging Religious," *Aging and Spirituality. Newsletter of the American Society on Aging's Forum on Religion and Aging* 3 (Winter, 1992), 2.

[5]Sherry Ruth Anderson and Patricia Hopkins, *The Feminine Face of God: The Unfolding of the Sacred in Women* (New York: Bantam Books, 1991), p. 49.

[6]See Ravenna Helson and Laurel McCabe, "The Social Clock Project in Middle Age," in *Women Growing Older: Psychological Perspectives*, p. 88.

[7]"Isabel Allende," in *On Women Turning 50: Celebrating Mid-Life Discoveries*, p. 166.

[8](New York: W.W. Norton & Company, 1981), p. 143.

[9]Quoted in *Songs of Experience: An Anthology of Literature on Growing Old*, p. 329.

[10]This is the term used by William Bridges in *Transitions* (Reading, MA: Addison-Wesley Publishing Company, 1980).

[11]Tenth Anniversary Edition (New York: W.W. Norton & Company, 1986), pp. 181–182. Helpful treatments of the spiritual dimensions of the mid-life transition are Janice Brewi and Anne Brennan, *Mid-Life: Psychological and Spiritual Perspectives* (New York: Crossroad Publishing Company, 1982); L. Patrick Carroll and Katherine Marie Dyckman, *Chaos or Creation: Spirituality in Mid-Life* (Mahwah, NJ: Paulist Press, 1986); and Sheila Murphy, *Mid-life Wanderer: The Woman Religious in Mid-life Transition* (Whitinsville: Affirmation Books, 1983).

[12]*The Awful Rowing Toward God* (Boston: Houghton Mifflin Company, 1975), pp. 15–16.

[13]*Candles in Babylon* (New York: New Directions Books, 1982), p. 97.

[14](New York: Harper & Row, 1978), pp. 193–194.

[15](New York: New American Library, 1986).

[16]Marilyn Zuckerman, "After Sixty," in *Poems of the Sixth Decade* (Cambridge, MA: Garden St. Press, 1993), p. 9. A helpful guide to the many dimensions of menopause is Joan C. Borton, *Drawing from the Women's Well: Reflections on the Life Passage of Menopause* (San Diego, CA: LuraMedia, 1992).

3. Tending the Inner Life

[1]In *If I Had My Life to Live Over I Would Pick More Daisies*, ed. Sandra Martz (Watsonville, CA: Papier-Mache Press, 1993), p. 171.

[2]Twentieth Anniversary Edition (New York: Random House, Inc., 1978), p. 87.

[3]The implications of this are explored in Alice Miller, *The Drama of the Gifted Child: The Search for the True Self*, trans. Ruth Ward (New York: Basic Books, 1981).

[4]"Ellen Burstyn," in *On Women Turning 50: Celebrating Mid-Life Discoveries*, p. 18.

[5]Delese Wear, "A Reconnection to Self: Women and Solitude," in *The Center of the Web: Women and Solitude*, ed. Delese Wear (Albany: State University of New York Press, 1993), pp. 3–11.

[6]*Tell Me a Riddle* (New York: Dell Publishing Company, 1961), pp. 1–2.

[7](San Francisco: Harper and Row, 1952), p. 285.

[8]Two helpful guides to this method of prayer are Thelma Hall, *Too Deep for Words: Rediscovering Lectio Divina* (Mahwah, NJ: Paulist Press, 1988); and William H. Shannon, *Seeking the Face of God* (New York: The Crossroad Publishing Company, 1988).

[9]See Thelma Hall, *Too Deep for Words*, p. 44.

[10](New York: The Viking Press, 1978), pp. 124–125.

[11]P. 131.

[12]P. 20.

[13](New York: Harcourt Brace Jovanovich, 1974), p. XXIV.

[14](New York: Bantam Books, 1990), pp. 6–7.

[15]Louise Thornton, "A Journey of Transformation," in *Women of the 14th Moon: Writings on Menopause*, p. 336.

[16]See *Wisdom of the Heart: Working with Women's Dreams*, pp. 38–41.

[17](New York: St. Martin's Press, 1987), p. 39.

[18]See Robert A. Johnson, *Inner Work: Using Dreams and Active Imagination for Personal Growth* (San Francisco: Harper & Row, 1986), pp. 97–134.

4. The Ways of Wisdom

[1](New York: Parabola Books, 1987), p. 30. Harold G. Koenig presents research that supports the importance of spirituality to aging in *Aging and God: Spiritual Pathways to Mental Health in Midlife and Later Years* (New York: The Haworth Press, 1994).

[2]For a helpful introduction to the role of biblical Wisdom in women's spirituality, see Susan Cady, Marian Ronan, and Hal Taussig, *Sophia: The Future of Feminist Spirituality* (San Francisco: Harper & Row, 1986).

[3](New York: Harcourt Brace & Company, 1993), p. 194.

[4]P. 193.

[5]Simone Weil, *Waiting for God*, trans. Emma Craufurd (New York: Harper and Row, 1951), pp. 69 and 115.

[6]"One Hundred Gifts," in Charlotte Painter and Pamela Valois, *Gifts of Age* (San Francisco: Chronicle Books, 1985), p. 125.

[7]James Luguri, *To Make a World: One Hundred Haiku and One Waka* (For Information: Gregory Martin, 227 1/2 10th St., Berkeley, CA, 1987), pp. 74 and 27.

[8]"Barbara Eddy," in *On Women Turning 50: Celebrating Mid-Life Discoveries*, p. 98.

[9](San Francisco: Harper and Row, 1989). See especially pp. 3, 50, 121–122, 144–145.

[10]Thich Nhat Hanh, *Being Peace*, ed. Arnold Kotler (Berkeley, CA: Parallax Press, 1987), p. 5.

[11]"Ayya Khema," in Anne Bancroft, *Weavers of Wisdom: Women Mystics of the Twentieth Century* (New York: Penguin Books, 1989), pp. 114–117.

[12]*Touching Peace: Practicing the Art of Mindful Living*, ed. Arnold Kotler (Berkeley, CA: Parallax Press, 1992), pp. 11–12.

[13]*Present Moment, Wonderful Moment: Mindfulness Verses for Daily Living* (Berkeley, CA: Parallax Press, 1990), p. 36.

[14]*The Miracle of Mindfulness: A Manual on Meditation*, trans. Mobi Ho. Revised Edition (Boston: Beacon Press, 1987), p. 12.

[15]A fine discussion of this can be found in Anne Carolyn Klein, "Finding a Self: Buddhist and Feminist Perspectives," in *Shaping New Vision: Gender and Values in American Culture*, pp. 191–218.

[16]"Centering Prayer," *America* 156 (February 28, 1987), 169–183. Also helpful are M. Basil Pennington, *Centering Prayer: Renewing an Ancient Christian Prayer Form* (New York: Doubleday & Company, 1980); and Thomas Keating, *Open Mind, Open Heart: The Contemplative Dimension of the Gospel* (Amity, NY: Amity House, 1986).

[17]I develop this further in *The Inner Rainbow: The Imagination in Christian Life* (Ramsey, NJ: Paulist Press, 1983).

[18]This process is discussed in Anna-Maria Rizzuto, *The Birth of the Living God: A Psychoanalytic Study* (Chicago: The University of Chicago Press, 1979).

[19]For a helpful guide to praying with new images, see Bridget Mary Meehan, *Exploring the Feminine Face of God* (Kansas City, MO: Sheed and Ward, 1991). The significance of speech about God for all areas of Christian life is explored in Elizabeth A. Johnson, *She Who Is: The Mystery of God in Feminist Theological Discourse* (New York: The Crossroad Publishing Company, 1992).

[20]*Showings*, translated from the critical edition by Edmund Colledge, O.S.A. and James Walsh, S.J. (New York: Paulist Press, 1978), Long Text, Chapter 77, p. 330.

[21]Joan M. Nuth, "Two Medieval Soteriologies: Anselm of Canterbury and Julian of Norwich," *Theological Studies* 53 (1992), 636. See also Nuth's *Wisdom's Daughter: The Theology of Julian of Norwich* (New York: The Crossroad Publishing Company, 1991).

[22](New York: The Putnam Publishing Group, 1992), pp. 112, 139–140. The relationship between creativity and aging is explored by Mary Baird Carlsen in *Creative Aging: A Meaning-Making Perspective* (New York: W.W. Norton & Company, 1991).

[23]For insights into Sarah and other key biblical women, see Katheryn Pfisterer Darr, *Far More Precious Than Jewels: Perspectives on Biblical Women* (Louisville, KY: Westminster/John Knox Press, 1991).

[24]*Old Age* (New York: Parabola Books, 1987), pp. 28–29. I discuss the importance of humor in *Winter Grace: Spirituality for the Later Years* (Mahwah, NJ: Paulist Press, 1985), pp. 100–114.

[25]J. Cheryl Exum, "'You Shall Let Every Daughter Live': A Study of Exodus 1:8–2:10," in *The Bible and Feminist Hermeneutics. Semeia* 28, ed. Mary Ann Tolbert (Chico, CA: Scholars Press, 1983), pp. 63–82.

[26]Emphasis on this truth is one of the contributions of liberation theology. For a fine summary of the relationship between justice and spirituality see

Charlene Spretnak, *States of Grace: The Recovery of Meaning in the Postmodern Age* (San Francisco: HarperCollins Publishers, 1991), pp. 156–195.

[27]*By Little and By Little: The Selected Writings of Dorothy Day*, ed. Robert Ellsberg (New York: Alfred A. Knopf, 1983), p. 332.

[28]"Impasse and Dark Night," in *Women's Spirituality: Resources for Christian Development*, ed. Joann Wolski Conn (Mahwah, NJ: Paulist Press, 1986), pp. 287–311.

[29]*The Collected Works of St. John of the Cross*, trans. Kieran Kavanaugh and Otilio Rodriguez (Washington, D.C.: Institute of Carmelite Studies, 1973).

[30]Constance FitzGerald, "Impasse and Dark Night," p. 292.

[31]*The Collected Works of St. John of the Cross*, pp. 140–141 and 313–329. See also the insights of Kenneth Leech, *Soul Friend: The Practice of Christian Spirituality* (San Francisco, Harper & Row Publishers, 1977), pp. 160–167.

[32]For a fine discussion and comparison see Joann Wolski Conn, *Spirituality and Personal Maturity*, pp. 128–167.

5. Body as Sacred

[1]In *Poems of the Sixth Decade* (Cambridge, MA: Garden St. Press, 1993), p. 75.

[2]"Ruth Zaporah," in *On Women Turning 50: Celebrating Mid-Life Discoveries*, p. 59.

[3]Dhyani Ywahoo, "Renewing the Sacred Hoop," in *Weaving the Visions: New Patterns in Feminist Spirituality*, ed. Judith Plaskow and Carol P. Christ (San Francisco: Harper & Row, 1989), p. 274.

[4]Sherry Ruth Anderson and Patricia Hopkins, *The Feminine Face of God: The Unfolding of the Sacred in Women*, p. 91.

[5]See Rosemary Radford Ruether, *Gaia & God: An Ecofeminist Theology of Earth Healing* (San Francisco: HarperCollins, 1992), p. 4. Also helpful is *Ecofeminism and the Sacred*, ed. Carol J. Adams (New York: The Continuum Publishing Company, 1993).

[6]For further reflection on this see Sallie McFague, *The Body of God: An Ecological Theology* (Minneapolis: Fortress Press, 1993), pp. 16–17.

[7]See Fritjof Capra, *The Tao of Physics*.

[8]*Hildegaard of Bingen: Mystical Writings*, trans. Robert Carver, ed. Fiona Bowie and Oliver Davies (New York: Crossroad Publishing Company, 1990), p. 92.

[9]See Elizabeth A. Johnson, *She Who Is: The Mystery of God in Feminist Theological Discourse*, pp. 165–166.

[10]Barbara Macdonald with Cynthia Rich, *Look Me in the Eye: Old Women, Aging and Ageism* (San Francisco: Spinster, Ink, 1983), p. 19.

[11]*The Seattle Times*, September 19, 1993, A 18.

[12]Quoted in Sherry Ruth Anderson and Patricia Hopkins, *The Feminine Face of God*, p. 99.

[13](New York: Harcourt Brace & Company, 1983), p. 241. See also Marilyn Barrett, *Creating Eden: The Garden as a Healing Space* (San Francisco: HarperCollins, 1992).

[14]See C. Gilbert Romero, "Tradition and Symbol as Biblical Keys for a United States Hispanic Theology," in *Frontlines of Hispanic Theology in the United States*, ed. Allan Figueroa Deck (Maryknoll, New York: Orbis, 1992), pp. 41–61.

[15]From the film, "Minnie Remembers," by Donna Swanson. Quoted in Jane Porcino, *Growing Older, Getting Better: A Handbook for Women in the Second Half of Life*, p. 193.

[16]"Sex and the Elderly: No Laughing Matter in Religion," *Journal of Religion and Aging* 3 (Fall/Winter 1986), 141–152.

[17]Jane Porcino, *Growing Older, Getting Better*, p. 195.

[18]Beverly Wildung Harrison, "Human Sexuality and Mutuality," in *Christian Feminism: Visions of a New Humanity*, ed. Judith L. Weidman (San Francisco: Harper & Row, 1984), pp. 141–157.

[19]Barry Lopez, *Arctic Dreams: Imagination and Desire in a Northern Landscape* (New York: Bantam Books, 1986), p. 66.

[20]Julia Esquivel, *Threatened with Resurrection* (Elgin, IL: The Brethren Press, 1994). Parker Palmer offers detailed and insightful reflections on this poem in *The Active Life: Wisdom for Work, Creativity, and Caring* (San Francisco: HarperCollins, 1990), pp. 139–157.

[21]Ellen Glasgow, *The Woman Within* (New York: Harcourt, Brace and Company, 1954), pp. 289–290.

[22]In *Love in Full Bloom: The Many Faces of Love in the Golden Years*, ed. Margaret Fowler and Priscilla McCutcheon (New York: Ballantine Books, 1994), pp. 357–358. Historian Caroline Walker Bynum situates the medieval concern with material continuity and bodily resurrection in a modern context in *Fragmentation and Redemption: Essays on Gender and the Human Body in Medieval Religion* (New York: Zone Books, 1992), pp. 239–417.

[23](Chicago: The University of Chicago Press, 1993), p. 307.

6. Seasons of Mourning

[1]"Women and Nature: Time of the New Dawning," in *The Spiral Path: Essays and Interviews on Women's Spirituality*, ed. Theresa King O'Brien (St. Paul, MN: YES International Publishers, 1988), p. 163.

[2](New York: Farrar, Straus and Giroux, 1980), p. 154. There are many

books on grief and loss. Some helpful ones are *In the Midst of Winter: Selections from the Literature of Mourning*, ed. Mary Jane Moffat (New York: Random House, 1982); Alla Bozarth-Campbell, *Life Is Goodby, Life Is Hello: Grieving Well Through All Kinds of Loss* (Minneapolis: CompCare Publishers, 1982); and C.S. Lewis, *A Grief Observed* (New York: Seabury Press, 1961).

[3] *Final Harvest: Emily Dickinson's Poems*, ed. Thomas H. Johnson (Boston: Little, Brown and Company, 1961), p. 73.

[4] Toby Talbot, *A Book About My Mother* (New York: Farrar, Straus and Giroux, 1980), p. 178.

[5] Helen Vozenilek, *Loss of the Ground-Note: Women Writing About the Loss of Their Mothers* (Los Angeles: Clothespin Fever Press, 1992), p. 100.

[6] Anna Akhmatova, *Crucifixion*, from "Requiem 1935–1940," in *Anna Akhmatova: Poem Without a Hero*, trans. Lenore Mayhew and William McNaughton (Oberlin, Ohio: Oberlin College Press, 1989), p. 89.

[7] *Two-Part Invention: The Story of a Marriage* (Farrar, Straus and Giroux, 1988), p. 169.

[8] *Sister Thea Bowman, Shooting Star: Selected Writings and Speeches*, ed. Celestine Cepress (Winona, Minnesota: Saint Mary's Press, 1993), p. 128.

[9] *Icon of the Sun* (Seattle, WA: Tabula Rasa Press, 1993), p. 45.

[10] Very helpful reflections on these themes can be found in Wendy Farley, *Tragic Vision and Divine Compassion: A Contemporary Theodicy* (Louisville, Kentucky: Westminster/John Knox Press, 1990).

[11] Quoted in Judith Herman, *Trauma and Recovery* (New York: HarperCollins, 1992), p. 209.

[12] Elizabeth A. Johnson offers a fine treatment of this topic in *She Who Is: The Mystery of God in Feminist Theological Discourse*, pp. 246–272.

[13] (New York: W.W. Norton & Company, 1984), p. 10.

[14] (New York: W.W. Norton & Company, 1988), p. 124.

[15] (New York: W.W. Norton & Company, 1992), p. 45.

[16] P. 14.

[17] (New York: W.W. Norton & Company, 1993), p. 332.

[18] *Journeys By Heart: A Christology of Erotic Power* (New York: The Crossroad Publishing Company, 1988), p. 101.

[19] Carolyn Niethammer, *Daughters of the Earth: The Lives and Legends of American Indian Women* (New York: Macmillan Publishing Company, 1977), pp. 252–254.

[20] See Gertrud Mueller Nelson, *To Dance with God: Family Ritual and Community Celebration* (Mahwah, NJ: Paulist Press, 1986), pp. 221–230.

[21] See Elliott A. Norse, *Ancient Forests of the Pacific Northwest*, for a description of the many dimensions of this process.

[22] Translated by Edmund Colledge and James Walsh, Short Text, Chapter iv, p. 130; and Long Text, Chapters 68, p. 315; 32, p. 232; and 86, p. 342.

7. Remembrance and Redemption

[1]P. 5.

[2](Brattleboro, Vermont: The Stephen Greene Press, 1976), p. xiii.

[3]"Reflections on Elderhood: Interviews," in *Aging as a Spiritual Journey*, p. 234.

[4]I am indebted to Steen Halling, Jan Rowe, and their colleagues in the Seattle University Department of Psychology for their research on the meaning of forgiveness. See Lin Bauer, et al., "Exploring Self-Forgiveness," *Journal of Religion and Health* 31 (1992), 149–160; and Jan O. Rowe, et al., "The Psychology of Forgiving Another: A Dialogal Research Approach," in *Existential-Phenomenological Perspectives in Psychology: Exploring the Breadth of Human Experience*, ed. R.S. Valle and S. Halling (New York: Plenum Publishing Corporation, 1989), pp. 233–244.

[5]*Old Age*, p. 46.

[6]John Patton, *Is Human Forgiveness Possible? A Pastoral Care Perspective* (Nashville: Abingdon Press, 1985), p. 176.

[7]Clarissa Pinkola Estes, *Women Who Run with the Wolves* (New York: Ballantine Books, 1992), p. 370.

[8]In Alice Walker, *Goodnight Willie Lee, I'll See You in the Morning: Poems* (New York: Harcourt Brace Jovanovich, 1979), p. 53.

[9]Judith Herman provides an excellent description of the healing process for traumatic memories in *Trauma and Recovery*.

[10]Lin Bauer, et al., "Exploring Self-Forgiveness," p. 157.

[11](Seattle, WA: Broken Moon Press, 1992), pp. 223–224.

[12]Virginia Woolf, *Orlando* (New York: Harcourt Brace & Company, 1956), p. 78. See also Mary Carruthers, *The Book of Memory* (Cambridge: University Press, 1990).

[13]A helpful treatment of this and other aspects of reminiscence can be found in Edmund Sherman, *Reminiscence and the Self in Old Age* (New York: Springer Publishing Company, 1991). See also *The Uses of Reminiscence: New Ways of Working with Older Adults*, ed. Marc Kaminsky (New York: The Haworth Press, 1984).

[14]Rugh, Madeline M., "Creativity and Life Review in the Visual Arts: The Transformative Experience of Florence Kleinsteiber," *Generations* 15 (Spring 1991), 30.

[15]"Ellen Burstyn," in *On Women Turning 50: Celebrating Mid-Life Discoveries*, p. 15.

[16]Virginia Woolf, *To the Lighthouse* (New York: Harcourt Brace & Company, 1955), p. 240.

[17](New York: Bantam Books, 1980), p. 121.

[18]Audrey Borenstein, "In Transit: Notes from the Border," in *Women of the 14th Moon: Writings on Menopause*, p. 160.

[19]See *Reminiscence and the Self in Old Age*, p. 32.

[20](New York: Simon & Schuster, 1978), p. 256.

[21]*The Measure of My Days*, p. 42. See also Robert N. Butler, "The Life Review: An Interpretation of Reminiscence in the Aged," *Psychiatry* 26 (1963), 65–76; and Erik Erikson, *Identity: Youth and Crisis* (New York: W.W. Norton & Company, 1968), pp. 139–140.

[22](New York: New American Library, 1987), pp. 23, 162. For an excellent discussion of memory and narrative in *Beloved* and in other works by women see Gayle Greene, "Feminist Fiction and the Uses of Memory," *Signs: Journal of Women in Culture and Society* 16 (1991), pp. 290–321.

8. Giving and Receiving Care

[1]Nel Noddings, *Caring: A Feminine Approach to Ethics and Moral Education* (Berkeley: University of California Press, 1984), p. 175.

[2]See Gail R. O'Day, "John," in *The Women's Bible Commentary*, pp. 302–303.

[3](New York: W.W. Norton & Company, 1989).

[4]Florida Scott Maxwell, *The Measure of My Days*, p. 32.

[5]Nel Noddings, *Caring*, p. 28.

[6]See Elaine M. Brody, "Parent Care as a Normative Family Stress," *The Gerontologist* 25 (1985), 19–28.

[7](Maryknoll, NY: Orbis Books, 1991).

[8]See pp. 132–147. Some helpful books on the practical dimensions of caregiving are Donna Cohen and Carl Eisdorfer, *Seven Steps to Effective Parent Care* (New York: G.P. Putnam Sons, 1993); Pat Herrington and Jim Ewens, *Hospice, A Special Kind of Caring: Handbook for Families Facing a Terminal Illness* (Milwaukee, WI: Milwaukee Hospice Home Care, 1991); and Nancy R. Hooyman and Wendy Lustbader, *Taking Care of Aging Family Members: A Practical Guide* (New York: The Free Press, 1986).

[9]"A New Crisis," in *Daughters of the Elderly: Building Partnerships in Caregiving*, ed. Jane Norris (Bloomington: Indiana University Press, 1988), p. 5.

[10]P. 180.

[11]Virginia L. Marlow, "Love Enough to Let Go," in *Daughters of the Elderly*, p. 194.

[12]*Two-Part Invention: The Story of a Marriage*, p. 128.

[13]See Judith V. Jordan, "Empathy and Self Boundaries," and "The Meaning of Mutuality," in *Women's Growth in Connection*, pp. 67–96.

[14]See Brody, "Parent Care as a Normative Family Stress," pp. 23–24.

[15]Beverly Wildung Harrison makes this point in "The Power of Anger in the Work of Love," in *Making the Connections: Essays in Feminist Social Ethics*, ed. Carol S. Robb (Boston: Beacon Press, 1985), p. 12.

[16]See Susan E. Foster and Jack A. Brizius, "Caring Too Much? American Women and the Nation's Caregiving Crisis," and Jessie Allen, "Caring Work and Gender Equity in an Aging Society," in *Women on the Front Lines: Meeting the Challenge of an Aging America*, pp. 47–73, and 221–239.

9. Legacies

[1](Kansas City, MO: Sheed and Ward, 1990), p. 4.

[2](New York: Ballantine Books, 1991), p. 526.

[3]I am grateful to Nell Martin, a participant in one of my Kirkridge workshops, for sharing this story of her mother with me.

[4]"Surviving the Blight," in *Inheriting Our Mothers' Gardens: Feminist Theology in Third World Perspective*, ed. Letty M. Russell, Kwok Pui-lan, Ada María Isasi-Díaz, and Katie Geneva Cannon (Philadelphia: The Westminster Press, 1988), pp. 75–90. See also *Double Stitch: Black Women Write About Mothers and Daughters*, ed. Patricia Bell-Scott, et al. (Boston: Beacon Press, 1991).

[5]Unpublished manuscript.

[6](New York: Kodansha International, 1993), p. 17.

[7]Quoted in Ada María Isasi-Díaz and Yolanda Tarango, *Hispanic Women: Prophetic Voice in the Church* (San Francisco: Harper & Row, 1988), p. 16.

[8](Berkeley, CA: Tonatiuh International, 1972), p. 4.

[9]See Gloria Ines Loya, "The Hispanic Woman: *Pasionaria* and *Pastora* of the Hispanic Community," in *Frontiers of Hispanic Theology in the United States*, ed. Allan Figueroa Deck, p. 128.

[10]Donald Conroy and Charles Fahey, "Christian Perspectives on the Role of Grandparents," in *Grandparenthood*, ed. Vern L. Bengtson and Joan F. Robertson (Beverly Hills, CA: SAGE Publications, 1985), p. 197. Also helpful is Carolyn Gutowski, *Grandparents Are Forever* (Mahwah, NJ: Paulist Press, 1994).

[11]Maggie Kuhn, quoted in Jane Porcino, *Growing Older, Getting Better: A Handbook for Women in the Second Half of Life*, p. 99.

[12]Daniel Berrigan wrote this in his introduction to Dorothy Day, *The Long Loneliness: An Autobiography* (San Francisco: Harper & Row, 1952), p. xxii.

[13]"Jubilee House—the Magic: An Interview with a Resident," *Newsletter of the Jubilee Women's Center* (Summer 1992), 1–2.

[14]Eva J. Salber, *Don't Send Me Flowers When I'm Dead: Voices of Rural Elderly* (Durham, NC: Duke University Press, 1983), p. 21.

[15]See Lorie Dwinell and Ruth Baetz, *We Did the Best We Could: How to Create Healing between the Generations* (Deerfield Beach, CA: Health Communications, Inc., 1993); Terry D. Hargrave and William T. Anderson, *Finishing Well: Aging and Reparation in the Intergenerational Family* (New York: Brunner-Mazil, 1992); and *Women in Families: A Framework for*

Family Therapy, ed. Monica McGoldrick, Carol M. Anderson, and Froma Walsh (New York: W.W. Norton & Company, 1989).

[16]For a sense of Craighead's creativity in the areas of imagery and ritual, see her *The Mother's Songs: Images of God the Mother* (Mahwah, NJ: Paulist Press, 1985); and *Litany of the Great River* (Mahwah, NJ: Paulist Press, 1991).

[17](Philadelphia: Fortress Press, 1987), p. 187.

[18]See Hildegard of Bingen, *Scivias*, pp. 190–191; and Gabriele Uhlein, *Meditations with Hildegard of Bingen*. A helpful source of other readings for inclusion in rituals is Marchiene Vroon Rienstra, *Swallow's Nest: A Feminine Reading of the Psalms* (Grand Rapids, MI: William B. Eerdmans Publishing Company, 1992).